pathfinder® guide

Cairngorms

WALKS

Compiled by
John Brooks, Neil Wilson and
Peter Koch-Osborne

Acknowledgements
The publisher would like to thank the Rothiemurchus Estate, the RSPB and Forest Enterprise for their considerable assistance in the preparation of this new edition.

Text:	John Brooks, Neil Wilson, Peter Koch-Osborne Revised text for 2005 edition, Hugh Taylor
Photography:	John Brooks, Neil Wilson, Peter Koch-Osborne
Editorial:	Ark Creative, Norwich
Design:	Ark Creative, Norwich
Series Consultant:	Brian Conduit

Jarrold Publishing ISBN 0-7117-0852-5

First published in 1996
Revised and reprinted 1999, 2002, 2005.
Printed in Belgium
by Proost NV, Turnhout. 4/05

Jarrold Publishing
Pathfinder Guides, Whitefriars, Norwich NR3 1TR
email: info@totalwalking.co.uk
www.totalwalking.co.uk

Front cover: The view from the rim of Coire an t-Sneachda
Previous page: Loch Muick

Contents

Short, easy walks

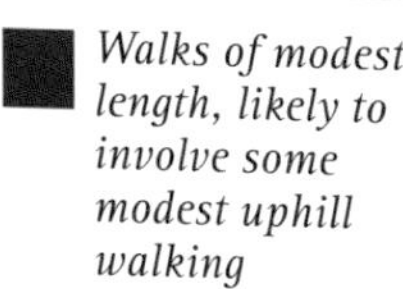
Walks of modest length, likely to involve some modest uphill walking

More challenging walks which may be longer and/or over more rugged terrain, often with some stiff climbs

Keymap 1

Auchgourish
Tulloch
Lodge
Braes of Abernethy
2257
Carn na Farraidh
Dalfaber
1465
Meall a' Bhuachaille
Carn Bheadhair
2692 Geal Charn
2636
2654
Coylumbridge
Glenmore Forest Park
The Queen's Forest
Glenmore
Cnap Chaochan Aitinn
2337
19
12
18
2435
Stac na h-Iolaire
Carn na Feannaige 2395
2431
Big Garvoun
Rothiemurchus
GLEN MORE
GLEN AVON
Carn Eilrig 2435
Castle Hill 2366
Bynack More 3574
2338
The Bruach
Forest of Glenavon
CAIRN GORM 4084
2932
Stob an t-Sluichd 3621
Lairig Ghru
CAIRNGORM MOUNTAINS
3983
Shelter Stone
Beinn a' Chaorainn 3553
3843
BEN AVON
Sgòran Dubh Mór 3635
Braeriach
4248
4296
3924
BEINN A'BHUIRD
3658
Sgòr Gaoith
4149
BEN MACDUI
3788 Derry Cairngorm
Dubh-Ghleann
3556 Carn Eas
GRAMPIAN MOUNTAINS
2830 Creag an Dail Bheag
4236
Cairn Toul
3051 Beinn Bhreac
3303 The Devil's Point
3329 Carn a' Mhaim
Carn na Drochaide
Monadh Mór 3651
Glen Dee
BRAEMAR
2681
Beinn Bhrotain 3795
Glen Lui
Creag Bhaig
Allanaquoich
Braemar
Castle
Sgòr Mór 2667
FOREST OF MAR
15
21
Mar Lodge
Muir Cottage
Muir
Inverey
2819
Auchallater
Cairn Geldie 2039
The Colonel's Bed
Glen Ey
Carn Liath 2676
Geldie Burn
2204
Carn an Fhidhleir or Carn Ealar
Glen Callater
Creag nan Gabhar 2736
3276
3300 An Sgarsoch
Carn Bhac 3014
3098
2989
Baddoch
2908 Sgòr Mór
2605
An Socach
3073
3340
Beinn Iutharn Mhór 3424
Carn a' Gheoidh 3194
3059
THE CAIRNWELL
Devil's Elbow
3504
Glas Maol
2882 Bràigh Sròn Ghorm
3377 Carn an Righ
Gleann Mór
Glas Tulaichean 3449
Caenlochan Forest
3238
Creag Leacach
3159
Forest Lodge
BEINN A' GHLO
3673
Glen Loch
2377
2641
Dalmunzie House Hotel
Ben Gulabin
2470
Carn an Daimh
Glen Tilt
2846 Meall a' Choire Bhuidhe
Spittal of Glenshee
3201 Carn Liath
2962
Ben Vuirich
Loch Valigan
2632 Ben Earb
Gleann Fearnach
Mealna Letter or 2301
Duchray Hill
2600 Meall Uaine
Creag an t-Sithein
Loch Moraig
Bridge of Tilt
Lude House
Blair Atholl
Dalnaglar Castle
1879 Lamh Dearg
Lair
Cray
Mount Blair 2442
Brewlands Bridge
Glen Shee
Balvarran
Ashintully Castle
Bonskeid House
Pass of Killiecrankie
2092 Creag Dhubh
Kirkmichael
Blacklunans

SCALE 1:250 000 or 1 INCH to 4 MILES *1CM to 2.5KM*

0 2 4 6 8 10 KILOMETRES 15

0 2 4 6 MILES 8 10

KEYMAP HEIGHTS SHOWN IN FEET

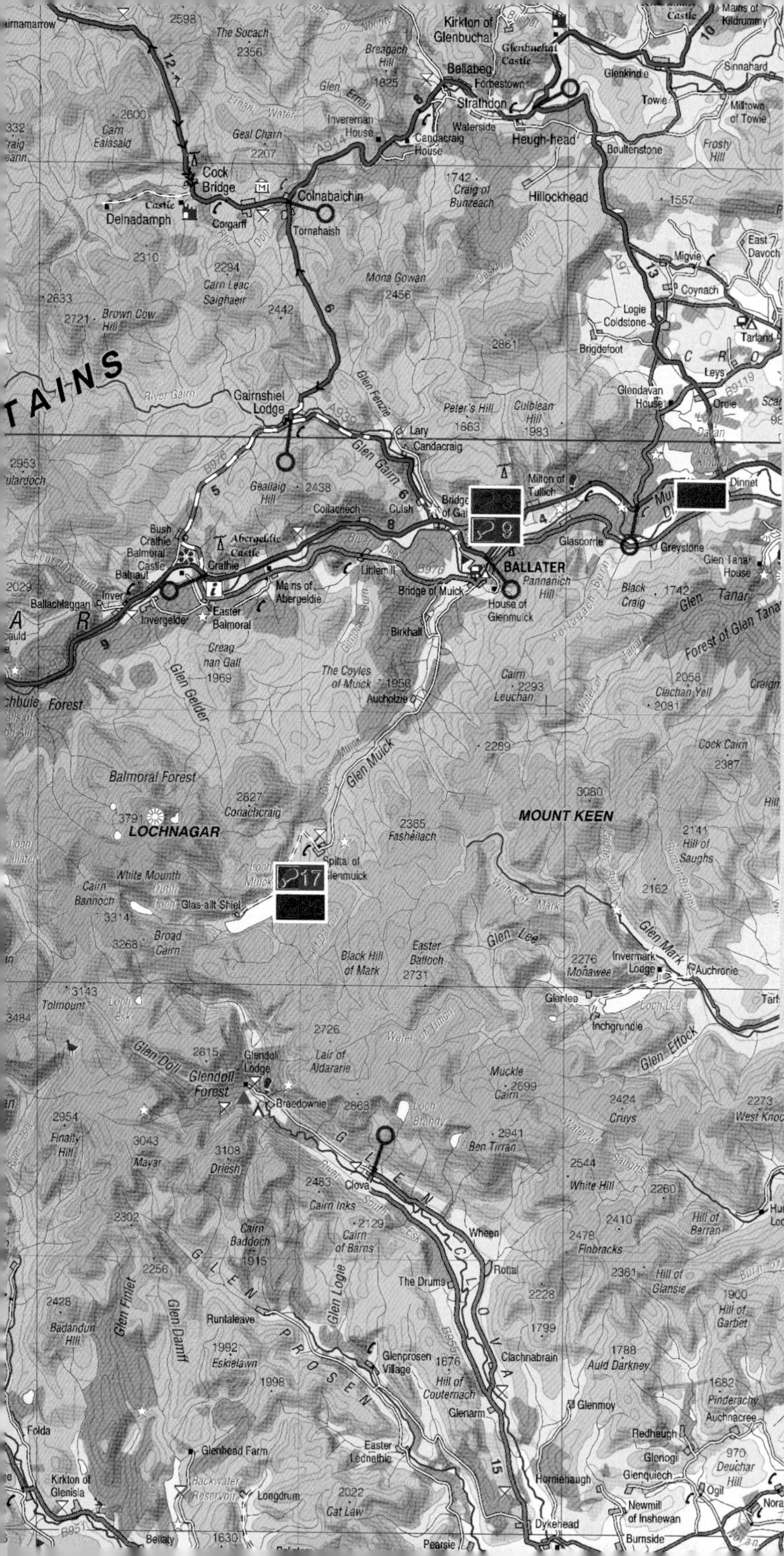

Keymap 1

Kirkton of Glenbuchat
Glenbuchat Castle
Mains of Kildrummy
The Socach
2598
2356
Breagach Hill
1825
Bellabeg
Forbestown
Strathdon
Glenkindie
Sinnahard
Towie
Milltown of Towie
Glen Ernan
Invererman House
Candacraig House
Waterside
Heugh-head
Boultenstone
Frosty Hill
Carn Ealasaid
2600
Geal Charn
2207
Cock Bridge
Delnadamph
Castle
Corgarff
Colnabaichin
Tornahaish
1742
Craig of Bunzeach
Hillockhead
1557
East Davoch
Migvie
Coynach
Logie Coldstone
Tarland
2310
2294
Carn Leac Saighaeir
Mona Gowan
2456
2442
2633
2721
Brown Cow Hill
2861
Bridgefoot
Leys
CROMAR
TAINS
River Gairn
Gairnshiel Lodge
Glen Fenzie
Peter's Hill
1863
Culblean Hill
1983
Glendavan House
Ordie
Loch Davan
Loch Kinord
Lary
Candacraig
Glen Gairn
2953
Geallaig Hill
2438
Milton of Tullich
Dinnet
Bridge of Gairn
Coilacriech
Culsh
Bush
Crathie
Balmoral Castle
Abergeldie Castle
Glascorrie
Greystone
Glen Tanar House
Balnault
Inver
Ballachlaggan
Invergelder
Easter Balmoral
Mains of Abergeldie
Littlemill
River Dee
Bridge of Muick
BALLATER
House of Glenmuick
Pannanich Hill
Black Craig
1742
Glen Tanar
Forest of Glen Tanar
2029
Birkhall
Creag nan Gall
1969
Glen Gelder
The Coyles of Muick
1956
Aucholzie
Cairn Leuchan
2293
2058
Clachan Yell
2081
Ballochbuie Forest
2289
Cock Cairn
2387
Balmoral Forest
2827
Conachcraig
3791
LOCHNAGAR
Glen Muick
3080
MOUNT KEEN
2365
Fasheilach
2141
Hill of Saughs
Spittal of Glenmuick
Loch Muick
White Mounth
Cairn Bannoch
3314
Dubh Loch
Glas-allt Shiel
2162
Water of Mark
Glen Mark
3268
Broad Cairn
Black Hill of Mark
Easter Balloch
2731
Glen Lee
2276
Monawee
Invermark Lodge
Auchronie
3143
Tolmount
Loch Esk
3484
Glenlee
Loch Lee
Inchgrundle
2726
Water of Unich
Lair of Aldararie
Glen Effock
Glen Doll
2815
Glendoll Lodge
Glendoll Forest
Braedownie
2863
Loch Brandy
Muckle Cairn
2699
2424
Cruys
2273
West Knock
2954
Finalty Hill
3043
Mayar
3108
Driesh
2941
Ben Tirran
2544
White Hill
2260
Hunthill Lodge
2483
Clova
Cairn Inks
GLEN CLOVA
River South Esk
2129
Cairn of Barns
Wheen
2410
Hill of Berran
2302
Cairn Baddoch
1915
2478
Finbracks
1759
Burn of Calletar
2256
Rottal
2381
Hill of Glansie
The Drums
2228
1900
Hill of Garbet
2428
Badandun Hill
Glen Finlet
Glen Damff
GLEN PROSEN
Glen Logie
Runtaleave
1799
Peat Hill
1992
Eskielawn
Glenprosen Village
1676
Clachnabrain
1788
Auld Darkney
1998
Hill of Couternach
1682
Pinderachy
Glenmoy
Glenarm
Auchnacree
1031
Tulloch Hill
Folda
Redheugh
Glenhead Farm
Easter Lednathie
Glenogil
970
Deuchar Hill
Kirkton of Glenisla
Backwater Reservoir
Longdrum
Glenquiech
Hornieheugh
Ogil
Fern
Noranside
2022
Cat Law
Newmill of Inshewan
Dykehead
Bellaty
1630
Burnside
Pearsie

Keymap 2

SCALE 1:250 000 or 1 INCH to 4 MILES *1CM to 2.5KM*

0 2 4 6 8 10 KILOMETRES 15

0 2 4 6 MILES 8 10

KEYMAP HEIGHTS SHOWN IN FEET

Keymap 2
Hill of Tomechole
Relugas
Redburn
Beachans
Airdre Mill
Ferness
Tomdow
River Divie
Dorback Burn
Loch Dallas
Carn na Cailliche
1324
Cairn Cattoch
1201
Robertstown
Archiestown
Pitchaish
Upper Knockando
Cardow
Knockando House
Knockando
Carron
Speyside Way
Daugh of Carron
Knock of Braemoray
1495
1712
Carn Kitty
Milltown
1783
Larig Hill
1692
Aitnoch
Dava
1318
Hill of Aitnoch
A939
B9007
Marypark
Belleheiglash
Ballindalloch Castle
Lochindorb
Lochindorb Lodge
1587
Carn Ruigh Chorrach
1800
Carn na Loine
Burn of Tulchan
Tormore
Advie
Bridge of Avon
760
A95
Dalchirach
Upper Derraid
Auchnagallin
Glenmore Loch
Lettoch
B9008
1605
Cairnacay
Craggan
Creag Liath
1473
Glaschoil
Lynmore
Cottartown
Camerory
Tomvaich
B9102
Dellefure
Mains of Dalvey
Drumin
Glenlivet
Shenval
Auchbreck
2330
Beinn Mhòr
1545
Dreggie
Glenbeg
Achnahannet
GRANTOWN-ON-SPEY
11
Cromdale
Haughs of Cromdale
HILLS OF CROMDALE
River Avon
Strath Avon
Carn Liath
1795
16
Dulnain Bridge
Craggan
A938
Speybridge
Congash
Carn Daimh
1866
Skye of Curr
Lynemore
2369
Creagan a' Chaise
Knockandhu
B9136
Broomhill Sta
A95
Sgòr Gaoithe
Easter Fodderletter
Clashnoir
B9008
Cullachie
Nethy Bridge
Dirdhu
Sliemore
Croughly
Speyside Way
Chapeltown
Birchfield
14
East Croftmore
Dell Lodge
Lettoch
Bridge of Brown
8
Boat of Garten
1863
Baddoch
1742
Tom an t-Suidhe Mhòr
Tomintoul
Milton
1924
Loch Garten
Forest
Aundorach
Tore Hill
Tulloch
Dorback Lodge
1982
Carn Meadhonach
Delnabo
A939
Forest Lodge
Braes of Abernethy
2267
Carn na Farraidh
Blairnamarrow
Meall a' Bhuachaille
Carn Bheadhair
2636
2692
Geal Charn
Water of Ailnack
River Avon
2654
Glenmore Forest Park
Queen's Forest
Glenmore
12
18
GLEN MORE
2435
Stac na h-Iolaire
Cnap Chaochan Aitinn
2337
2332
Craig Veann
Carn Ealasaid
Carn na Feannaige
2395
2431
Big Garvoun
AVON
Castle
Delnadamph
Castle Hill
2366
Bynack More
3574
2310
CAIRN GORM
4084
GLEN
2338
The Bruach
Forest of Glenavon
2633
2721
Brown Cow Hill
2932
Lairig Ghru
CAIRNGORM
3983
Shelter Stone
Beinn a' Chaorainn
3553
Stob an t-Sluichd
3621
3843
BEN AVON
River Gairn
3924
4296
MOUNTAINS
BEN MACDUI
3788
Derry Cairngorm
Dubh Ghleann
BEINN A' BHUIRD
Carn Eas
3556
2953
Culardoch
2830
Creag an Dail Bheag
4236
Cairn Toul
3051
Beinn Bhreac
GRAMPIAN MOUNTAINS
3303
The Devil's Point
3329
Carn a' Mhaim
Carn na Drochaide
Meall Gorm
2029
Bush
Crathie
Balmoral Castle
Balnault
Inver
Ballachlaggan
Invergelder
BRAEMAR
2681

Walk	Page	Start	Nat. Grid Reference	Distance	Time	Highest Point
The Braes of Abernethy	22	Dorback Lodge	NJ 077168	4½ miles (7.2km)	2½ hrs	1410ft (430m)
Bynack More from Glenmore	73	Allt Mor	NH 985074	14 miles (22.5km)	7 hrs	3575ft (1090m)
Cambus o' May and the Muir of Dinnet	66	Dinnet	NO 459987	9 miles (14.5km)	4½ hrs	984ft (300m)
Carn an Fhreiceadain	76	Kingussie	NH 755015	9½ miles (15.25km)	4 hrs	2880 ft (878m)
Carn Daimh from Glenlivet	48	Tomnavoulin	NJ 208265	6½ miles (10.5km)	3½ hrs	1870ft (570m)
Carrbridge and General Wade's Rd.	39	Carrbridge	NH 907227	7½ miles (12km)	3½ hrs	<1312ft (<400m)
Craigendarroch	18	Ballater	NO 366960	2½ miles (4km)	1½ hrs	1319ft (402m)
Creag a Chalamain and Castle Hill	37	Allt Mor	NH 985074	8½ miles (13km)	4½ hrs	2581ft (787m)
Creag Bheag and Loch Gynack	26	Kingussie	NH 755007	4 miles (6.5km)	2½ hrs	1598ft (487m)
Eag a' Chait and Loch Morlich	54	Loch Morlich	NH 957096	7 miles (11.25km)	4½ hrs	1860ft (568m)
Fiacaill and Cairn Lochan	60	Chairlift car park	NH 989060	6½ miles (10.5km)	4 hrs	3990ft (1215m)
Five Bridges Walk, Ballater	30	Ballater	NO 369958	5½miles (8.75km)	3 hrs	<1000ft (<300m)
Gleann Einich	70	Whitewell	NH 916086	12½ miles (20km)	6½ hrs	1640ft (500m)
Glen Banchor and Craggan	16	Glen Road, Newtonmore	NN 714992	3 miles (4.75km)	1½ hrs	1036ft (316m)
Glen Brown and Tom nam Marbh	28	White Bridge	NJ 132209	4½ miles (7.25km)	2 hrs	1350ft (410m)
Glen Feshie	33	Glen Feshie	NN 842996	6½ miles (10.5km)	3 hrs	1380ft (420m)
Glen Lui and Derry Lodge	45	Linn of Dee car park	NO 062897	7 miles (11.25km)	3 hrs	1380ft (420m)
Grantown-on-Spey	35	Grantown-on-Spey	NJ 035279	7 miles (11.25km)	3 hrs	656ft (200m)
The Lairig Ghru	83	Whitewell	NH 897084	12½ miles (20km)	7 hrs	1968ft (600m)
The Lily Loch and Loch an Eilein	24	Inverdruie	NH 901109	6 miles (9.7km)	3 hrs	1083ft (330m)
Linn of Quoich	20	Linn of Quoich	NO 118911	3 miles (4.75km)	2 hrs	1312ft (400m)
Loch an Eilein	57	Coylum Bridge	NH 913106	8 miles (12.75km)	3 hrs	984ft (300m)
Loch Garten and Loch Mallachie	14	2 miles east of Boat of Garten	NH 972186	1¾ miles (2.75km)	1 hr	744ft (220m)
Loch Muick	51	Spittal of Glen Muick	NO 309851	7½ miles (12km)	3½ hrs	1476ft (450m)
Lochnagar and Loch Muick	86	Spittal of Glen Muick	NO 309851	14 miles (22.5km)	7 hrs	3790ft (1155m)
Morrone	63	Braemar	NO 143910	7 miles (11.25km)	3½ hrs	2815ft (859m)
The Red Well	42	Newtonmore	NN 714992	6 miles (9.7km)	3 hrs	1480ft (450m)
Sron na Lairige and Braeriach	79	Loch an Eilein	NH 897084	18 miles (28.8km)	8–10 hrs	4057ft 1237m

< signifies 'less than'

Comments

Waterproof footwear is recommended on this walk which involves fording quite a few streams. It goes nowhere in particular but returns through sand dunes – unique in an inland walk.
This is a strenuous and demanding route which should be attempted only if the weather is good. Be prepared for rough walking over path and moorland. The views from the summit reward the effort.
The shallow lochs of Kinord and Davan at the start of this walk are rich in birdlife. They are followed by the pine and birch forests on Culblean Hill and the wooded banks of the River Dee.
The Monadhliath Mountains are part of the southern Grampians and face the Cairngorms across the Spey valley. The summit of Carn an Fhreiceadain gives fine views and a flavour of these desolate hills.
A walk on the Glenlivet Estate, climbing up through woodland and open country to the summit of Carn Daimh. It then drops back down with spectacular views across the glen.
Sluggan Bridge is a memorable beauty spot reached by part of General Wade's Road. The path can be wet and there is a stream to ford, so take waterproof footwear or be prepared to wade barefoot.
The climb starts in delightful woodland where red squirrels are common. The summit looks to Lochnagar in the south west, a view best seen in the low light of early morning or late summer evening.
The opening section of this walk takes advantage of newly-constructed and restored paths before reaching hill terrain. Beautiful woodland and forest paths are included for a delightful route.
Creag Bheag is an outstanding viewpoint for Strathspey, while the way back to Kingussie is along a path following the shore of Loch Gynack.
The highlights of this walk are the pass of Eag a' Chait with its grand views to the summits of the Cairngorms, and the ancient pine forest complete with reindeer.
Walk or take the chairlift for the first part of this route, then head for the rim of Coire an t-Sneachda corrie and the summit of Cairn Lochan.
Ballater's Victorian heyday is remembered in the magnificent station and several military memorials along this walk which passes through woods and criss-crosses the River Dee and its tributaries.
Gleann Einich is one of the finest of the Cairngorm glens, replete with red deer. This walk follows the burn right through its heart to the beautiful Loch Einich at its head.
Taken on a fine summer evening, this walk to Craggan offers views over the Spey valley to the Cairngorms beyond. It returns to the village of Newtonmore beside the waters of the River Calder.
On part of the Glenlivet Estate, this route is not accessible during the deer stalking season, but otherwise provides pleasant walking through open country with some woodland and waterside scenery.
Follow the path to one of the most beautiful waterfalls in the Cairngorms, set amongst pine trees below the peak of Carn Bàn Beag and above the calm of Glen Feshie.
This route affords fine views over Glen Lui to Derry Cairngorm and Ben Macdui, the second highest mountain in Britain. The walk is not suitable for younger children.
A gentle walk along the banks of the Spey, famous for its salmon, starts off through attractive woodland and finishes on one of General Wade's military roads.
A good walk for fine summer weather when the three passes of Lairig Ghru, the Chalamain Gap and Eag a' Chait should be free from snow. It also takes in the Rothiemurchus pine forest and the pretty Lochan Deò.
Take your lunch and sit by the Lily Loch with the mountains in the distance, or wander through the woods in the evening. Midge repellent is recommended – as with any lochside excursion.
An easy walk but care is still required as the paths can be wet and slippery and made uneven by tree roots. Red squirrels, sculpted rock and rushing water complement views to Morrone.
A peaceful walk around the far shores of Loch an Eilein, taking in fine woodland, mountain and lochside scenery without steep gradients.
The highlight of this short walk through woodland to lochs Garten and Mallachie is to see ospreys, but there are also rewards in the gentle gradients, beautiful scenery and great variety of birdlife.
Loch Muick was greatly loved by Queen Victoria, who often visited the waterfall at Glas Allt and picnicked on the sandy beach at the head of the loch.
This is a long but satisfying walk to the summit of Lochnagar and the Falls of the Glas Allt, taking in a circuit of Loch Muick.
The initial climb of 1600ft (490m) to the summit of Morrone gives staggering views of Deeside, Lochnagar and other Cairngorm summits. The bare moorland supports good flocks of grouse and mountain hares.
Don't attempt this walk in poor visibility – the path is faint. In any weather the way is bleak but nevertheless exhilarating crossing open moorland to the ancient Red Well.
This walk should be attempted only in the summer months and will require an early start. The route is long and arduous but is rewarded with stunning views of the Cairngorm plateau.

Introduction to the Cairngorms

The majority of people get their first view of the Cairngorms as they drive northwards up the A9 from Perth. At first the mountains lie low on the horizon, their great bulk disguised by distance. Later they grow to dominate the view ahead and serious walkers and climbers will feel elation as they view the dark corries rising gloriously and precipitously to craggy summits. The range covers about 300 sq miles (777 sq km) which make the Cairngorms the most extensive mountainous area to be found in Britain. Geologically it belongs to the Grampian mountain system, the massif which lies at the heart of the Scottish Highlands. The River Dee flows from the eastern side of the Cairngorms and separates Lochnagar from the other main summits. An important route through the Cairngorms, the Lairig Ghru, follows the Dee upstream to its source and then crosses the watershed below Ben Macdui to descend to Speyside. The road from Ballater to Grantown-on-Spey via Tomintoul provides a further boundary with Glenlivet (a district famous for its malt whiskies) and the Ladder Hills to the north east.

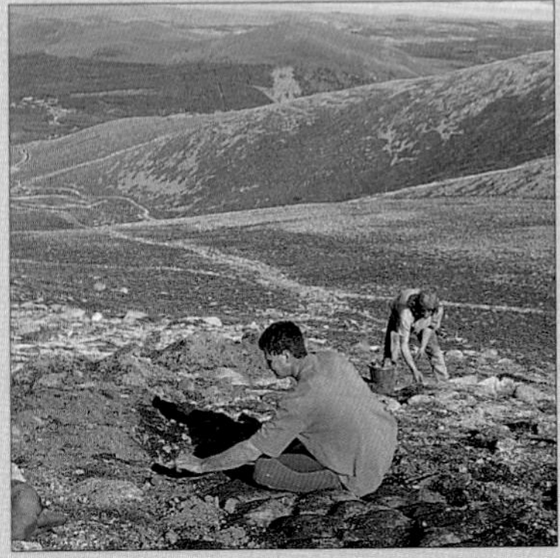

Footpath repairs on the way to Fiacaill

The A9 from Perth to Inverness follows the course of the River Spey and separates the Cairngorms from more mountains to the west, the Monadhliaths. These are comparatively unspectacular heights, a succession of hills which rarely boast summit crags or easy access routes and are thus usually ignored by walkers. In contrast the Cairngorms rise imperiously to the east of the Spey, their tops often snow-covered and veiled by mist. This beauty has beguiled many walkers and climbers over the years into disregarding the dangers and some have suffered accordingly. The Cairngorms should never be taken lightly so take heed of the warnings which follow.

Words of Caution

This book includes routes which could pose problems to those unaccustomed to walking in high and lonely places. On the high Cairngorm plateau the weather can pose severe problems. A bright and sunny day at lower levels can become less agreeable after you have climbed a thousand or so feet (300m). While people sunbathe on Loch

Morlich's beaches it can be blowing a blizzard on the mountain plateau less than four miles (6.5km) away. Mist is potentially a killer once you become lost and some paths are difficult to see even in perfect conditions. In springtime and early summer deep snow lingers in many places and is particularly dangerous when it covers rough ground. Rotten snow gives way without warning and even a short fall can break a leg or an ankle. Fresh snow causes more obvious problems, especially if it is driven by a gale-force wind so that it is hardly possible to see further than an outstretched hand. At such times it is essential to know exactly where you are and which direction to take to reach safety. Never go to the Cairngorm tops without adequate warm, waterproof clothing, maps, compass, whistle, emergency rations and a first-aid kit. Practise using map and compass in good conditions at a place where you know the landmarks and be sure to hear a weather forecast before deciding to tackle any route taking you higher than about 2500 ft (762m). It is also sensible to tell family and friends where you plan to walk each day. The Mountaincall telephone forecast for the East Highlands is 09068 500442.

Moss campion — a flower of the tundra

Vegetation and Geology

The Cairngorm vegetation reflects the varied climates encountered as you climb higher at this latitude. The river valleys are comparatively verdant and well wooded. Loch Morlich, at about 1000 ft (300m) above sea level, is surrounded by pine trees and has sandy beaches where people lie and sunbathe in the summer. The characteristic vegetation of the ancient Caledonian forest, Scots' pines with underlying juniper bushes and blaeberries, is encountered up to a height of about 1600 ft (487m) though at this altitude the junipers will have disappeared and the pines will be very stunted. Rothiemurchus means 'the plain of the great pine', and the forest is one of the last areas of naturally regenerating pine forest in Britain. It may also claim to be the most beautiful, with birches mingling with the Scots' pines at low levels making the forest particularly beautiful in the autumn, especially where it fringes the lochs.

Heather will easily survive this high but becomes sparse above 2500 ft (762m) by which time the characteristic sub-arctic tundra vegetation of the plateau will have taken over with mat grass, three-leaved and sedge rush as well as dwarf willow and various mosses. There is also reindeer moss *(Cladonia rangiferina)* which helps to support the herd of reindeer introduced into the Cairngorms 45 years ago, and examples of Alpine flora like starry saxifrage and moss campion whose flowers are such a surprise on the bare, pink granite. This rose-coloured rock is the main bedrock of the highland area. One of the most ancient rocks to be found in Britain, it burst from the core of the earth like a molten fist and solidified as it cooled. The great heat produced in this plutonic episode altered surrounding rock and also created 'cairngorms', beautiful smoky gemstones with colours ranging from yellow through red to black. Later geological activity, about 500 million years ago, distorted the granitic intrusion and the surrounding strata, but the granite remained at the core of the system through the millennia, gradually being reduced by the elements. In recent geological time, during the Ice Age, glaciers gouged out great corries at the start of their course from the tops of the mountains, flowed down to chisel distinctive U-shaped valleys, and ended by dumping debris to form morraines, glacial lakes and so on as they melted.

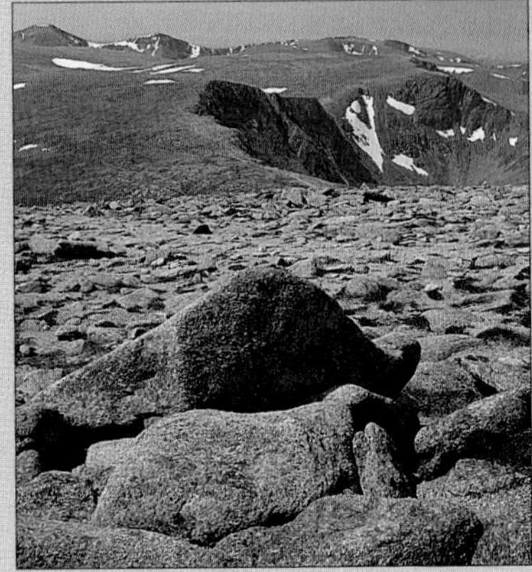

The summit of Cairn Gorm

Wildlife

The variety of countryside found in the district provides an equally wide range of habitats for wildlife. The native pine forest supports small uncommon birds like crested tits, redwings and crossbills, with siskins comparatively common. This is one of the final retreats of the native red squirrel and these delightful animals appear to be shy of humans but not of dogs. They delight in swearing at dogs from the safety of a tree when they have been disturbed in their foraging. Deer only roam in the lower parts of the forest in midwinter when food is scarce elsewhere.

Of the birds of prey, the osprey steals the limelight from the golden eagle in the Cairngorms. The RSPB's breeding site on Loch Garten is nationally famous and in summer the ospreys overfly a considerable tract of country in search of food. Equally attractive is the peregrine falcon which has a well-known breeding site amongst the crags of Craigellachie overlooking Aviemore. In many other parts of Britain the peregrine has suffered from pesticide poisoning but it appears to escape this in north east Scotland.

The mountain tops provide an environment akin to that of the arctic so it is hardly surprising that the species of northern latitudes should flourish. The snow bunting nests amongst the boulders on the plateau while the dotterel prefers smoother ground. The ptarmigan is probably the best known of all the mountain birds of the Cairngorms though you will be very fortunate to see one even though, like the dotterel, it nests on bare rock.

Lower down the mountain, where the vegetation is more abundant, game birds like red and black grouse and, much more rarely, capercaille will be found. Stocks of the latter are very depleted, probably because it is a large bird which doesn't fly very well – it has been described as a flying turkey. Mountain hares are particularly abundant on moorland to the west of the Spey but may be encountered almost anywhere. They run beautifully, sometimes pausing and standing on back legs to look for signs of pursuit. Their blue-grey coats turn white in winter.

Footnotes

This brings us to points which affect walkers in the area today. Long 'walk-ins' to the mountains are a characteristic of the Cairngorms. Many of the most famous routes are long linear excursions which use mountain passes to cross the watershed from Speyside to Deeside. Road access to the passes is restricted so that often it takes two or three hours' walking before the landscape becomes notably mountainous. The low level walks can be tackled at any time of year, but the higher you go the more circumspect you should be. None of the longer, higher routes should be undertaken until early summer. The Lairig Ghru keeps its snowfields into June, and since they cover streams and boulder fields this is one of the routes best left until the snow has completely melted. There is a magical short time when you can walk almost anywhere on the plateau without treading on snow yet still see it clinging to north-facing corries and crevices. July, still with long days, is a good time for walking even though the infernal midge begins to become active near most lochs. August sees the beginning of the grouse season which brings restrictions on access to some areas and this continues until December, though the most important shoots take place at the beginning of this period.

Goldfinches love the pine forests

Deer stalking takes place between mid-August and mid-October when red deer stags are in prime condition. If a cull did not take place the over-population of deer would lead to great suffering by the animals and harm to farmland as they desperately tried to find food in winter. Stalking brings some restrictions to walkers who will obviously not want to get in the way of a high velocity bullet. Take heed of notices and if possible telephone the estate you will be walking over to make sure that the date is clear. Where possible, relevant telephone numbers are given in the text for the walks while tourist information offices usually have up-to-date details of restrictions. A selection of useful numbers is listed on p.95.

Loch Garten and Loch Mallachie

Start	2 miles (3.25km) east of Boat of Garten
Distance	1¾ miles (2.75km)
Approximate time	1 hour
Parking	RSPB car park for woodland walks (not the one for the ospreys)
Refreshments	None
Ordnance Survey maps	Landranger 36 (Grantown & Aviemore), Explorer 403 (Cairngorm & Aviemore)

This is a very short walk into the RSPB's reserve at Loch Garten famous for its nesting ospreys (though the hide for observing the nest site is about ½ mile/800m to the east and is reached from a different car park). There is always the possibility of seeing one of the ospreys flying to or from the nest while on this walk which takes you to the shores of a pair of beautiful lochs, with views of the long ridge of the Kincardine Hills beyond.

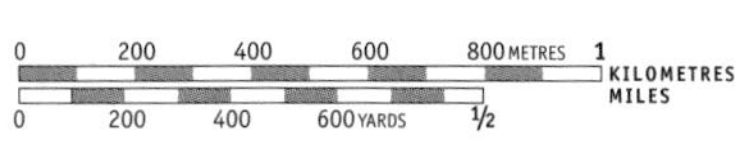

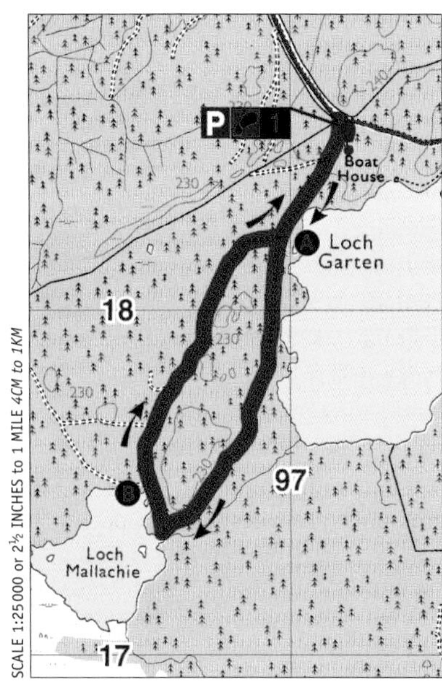

From the RSPB car park take the green trail through the forest. This is part of Abernethy Forest, the largest area of native pinewoods in Scotland. The RSPB reserve now covers over 31,000 acres (12,545 ha) and is renowned for its ospreys – birds of prey living primarily from fishing – which have bred here since 1959.

Many of the other species of birds to be seen in the reserve may lack the glamour and publicity value of the ospreys but are still of great interest to ornithologists.

Loch Garten **A** is reached in about five minutes and you then follow a lovely shoreline path. The loch is fringed by pine trees and heather, and the western summit of the Kincardine Hills, Craiggowrie, draws the eye to the south. In the autumn and winter

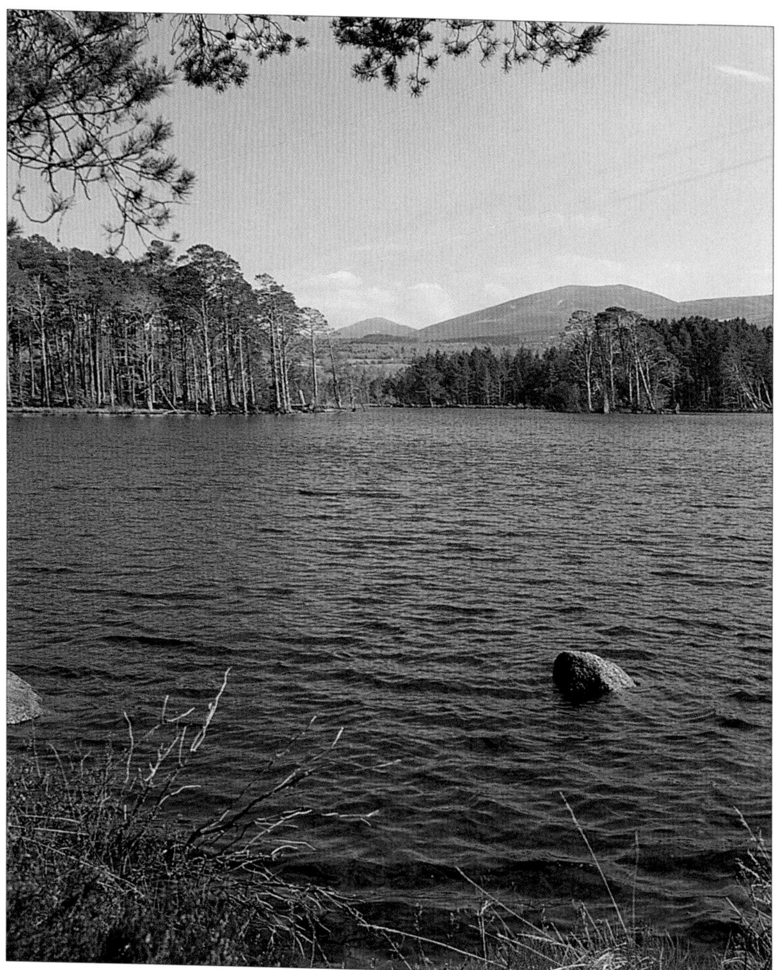

Loch Mallachie

wildfowl come to roost here at night, including large flocks of greylag geese and goosanders.

The path leaves Loch Garten and goes through a short section of forest before coming to Loch Mallachie which is even more beautiful with exceptionally straight, tall pine trees. There is a beautiful island with eight trees just offshore and many delightful spots to linger if you follow the shore round beyond a footpath junction ●. The large boxes visible on the two islands are used by goldeneyes, the male distinctive in black and white plumage with a white spot below each eye. The female lacks this spot and has a brown head. Goldeneyes rarely nest in Britain and it is estimated that a quarter of the British population is to be found on this reserve.

From ● keep ahead to follow the trail markers bearing green/blue blazes through the forest. Woodland birds to look out for here include crested tits, siskins and Scottish crossbills. The forest also supports red squirrels. In about ten minutes you reach the outward part of the route and in another five you will be back at the car park. ●

Glen Banchor and Craggan from Newtonmore

Start	Glen Road, Newtonmore
Distance	3 miles (4.75km)
Approximate time	1½ hours
Parking	Car parks on Glen Road before church. The one nearest the church is reserved for churchgoers on Sundays
Refreshments	Pubs and café in Newtonmore
Ordnance Survey maps	Landranger 35 (Kingussie & Monadhliath Mountains) and Explorer 402 (Badenoch & Upper Strathspey)

This short walk, which makes a delightful evening stroll, wanders through pastures and woodland to Craggan, a fine viewpoint above the upper reaches of the Spey valley. The return follows the river, and on hot evenings the air will resound to the shrieks and screams of children bathing in the refreshing waters of the infant Spey as it twists through a wooded gorge at the start of its long journey to the North Sea.

■ Glen Road begins from Newtonmore's main street opposite the war memorial and village hall. Walk past the church and at a house named Ardnabruach turn right to follow a signpost to Craggan. At the end of the road go through a gate and walk to the top of a field where there is another gate. From here the path ascends to join an ancient grooved track ● which curves around the flank of the hill through a beautiful birch wood.

This track joins another at a gate and this in turn then curves left and becomes grassy as it leads to a second gate at the side of a white house. Do not go through this gate but turn left and walk through the trees for five minutes until you reach the Craggan viewpoint ●. This lovely spot gives views over the village and the Spey valley to the Cairngorms to the east.

Newtonmore from Craggan

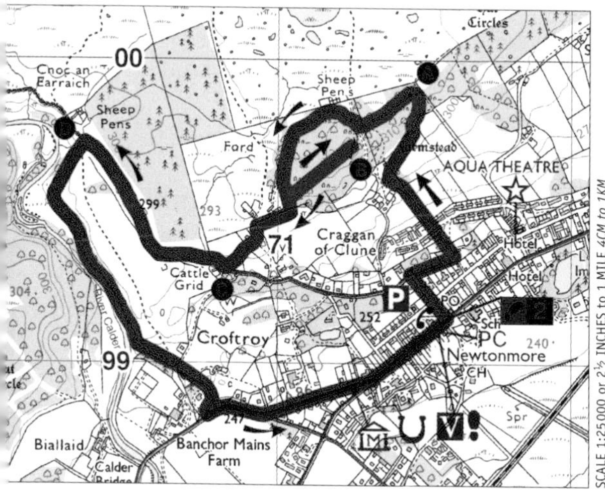

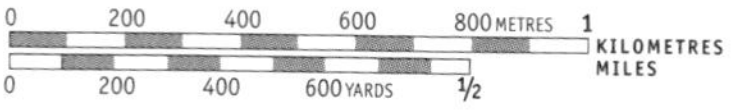

Newtonmore grew up because of its strategic position on General Wade's military road which crossed the Corrieyairack Pass to reach Inverness. It grew in size after tenants in Glen Banchor were moved from their crofts to the village to make way for sheep. The poverty which was in evidence at that time lead to its being described by Queen Victoria as 'a very long poor village'.

Today its situation by the main railway line and trunk road makes it important as a tourist centre. The Clan Macpherson museum at Newtonmore has many mementoes of the clan's ardent support for the Stewart cause during the campaigns of 1715 and 1745. The Chief was a fugitive in these parts for eight years after Culloden, using hideouts close to the then newly built Cluny Castle, the clan headquarters, before managing to escape to France. The castle was torched by government supporters but was rebuilt and was one of the Highland properties which Queen Victoria considered before she settled at Balmoral. Unhappily the Macphersons left it more than 50 years ago. The annual gathering of the Clan Macpherson takes place at Newtonmore and Kingussie over the first weekend in August.

Return to the white house (Upper Knock) from the viewpoint and keep it to the left as you walk round it to a track. Turn left on to this and follow it down through a birch wood to join Glen Road by a cattle grid ●. Turn right following a sign pointing to Glen Banchor.

A short stretch of road follows over open moorland and this gradually descends to a spot where there are seats on the left ●. Turn left off the road on to a path which follows the eastern side of the beautiful wooded glen. The River Calder flows through a gorge with waterfalls and deep pools, the latter making good bathing places in hot weather. Eventually the path reaches a burial ground and then goes through a kissing-gate to join a lane. A famous sign, written in Gaelic, points to the burial ground. In English it means 'The road established by law to St Bride's graveyard' and it was put up in 1876 after a farmer had attempted to build over the path. The graveyard takes its name from an anchorite's cell situated here dedicated to Brigid of Kildare who lived in the 6th century and was canonised as St Bride. Robert Louis Stevenson is supposed to have been inspired to write *Catriona* while contemplating a gravestone here.

When the lane from the burial ground meets the main road turn left to return to Newtonmore. ●

Craigendarroch

Start	Craigendarroch Walk, Ballater
Distance	2½ miles (4km)
Approximate time	1½ hours
Parking	On road at start
Refreshments	Pubs and cafés in Ballater
Ordnance Survey maps	Landranger 44 (Ballater & Glen Clova), Explorer 405 (Aboyne, Alford & Strathdon)

Craigendarroch ('the rocky hill of the oak wood') is the steep granite hill dominating Ballater from the north. Although only just over 1300ft (400m) high it is nevertheless one of Deeside's finest viewpoints. The crag is best climbed early or late in the day, when Lochnagar's crags and corries are lit by low light which also warms the foliage of the trees on the hills and along the riverbanks.

Craigendarroch Walk is the name given to a new housing development on the western side of Ballater, situated about ¼ mile (400m) from the town centre on the A93.

Two waymarked routes start from here – a circular route which follows yellow-topped posts, and the 'Over the Top' walk which has blue-topped posts. The starting point of these routes is clearly marked at the beginning of the road and there is no problem in parking nearby on the straight stretch of the road.

The path climbs behind the new houses through lovely woods of oak, birch and pine. After a little way the path drops down to join another one, and then climbs again and passes a seat. A little further on there is a large stone set in the middle of the path. Turn left here following the sign on a birch tree 'To Top and Round'. The path climbs up steeply to pass below a rock face. Oak trees become fewer as height is gained and rowans, pines and birches more plentiful. Red squirrels are comparatively commonplace here, and if you are walking with a dog they will take to the treetops and swear loudly. The woods are rich in a

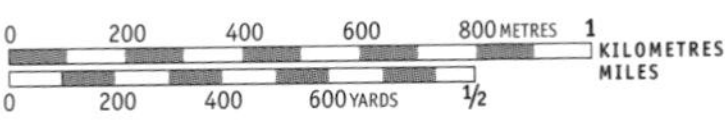

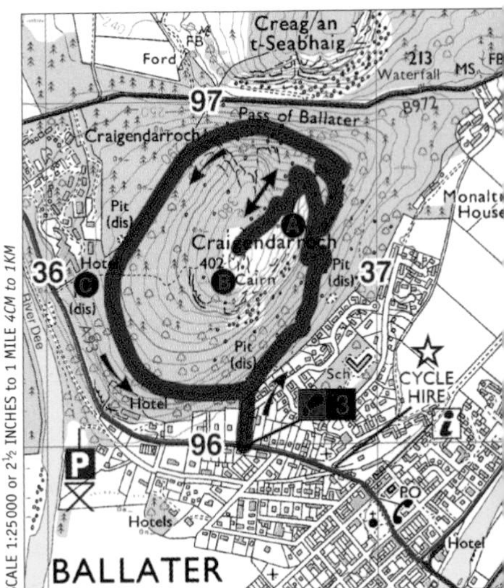

The view from Craigendarroch

wide variety of fungi in late summer and autumn.

At the end of the rock face the path comes to a seat and here the way divides ●. Turn left here to climb to the summit of Craigendarroch. The path is steep and ascends a series of rocky staircases which are well maintained. There are very few places where you would get your feet wet. It will take about 30 minutes to reach the top from the start of the walk. A large cairn ● overlooks Ballater and its large caravan site. However, in all other directions the vistas are superb, with Lochnagar distinct to the south west.

From the summit there is a choice of routes. If time is limited you may prefer to descend from the cairn westwards, following the blue-topped posts. Better still, retrace your steps to ● – which will take about ten minutes – and then turn left on to the circular route. This soon gives views of the impressive pink rockface on the far side of the Pass of Ballater – called Creag an t-Seabhaig, 'the precipice of the hawk' – and you may well see climbers negotiating its cracks and crevices.

The path zigzags down and occupies a narrow ledge above a precipitous slope before entering a plantation of mature pine trees to pursue a less exciting course. It swings southwards and there is an old wall to the right. When this ends the path comes back to the mixed woodland seen at the start of the walk. The direct route from the summit cairn rejoins beside a magnificent Scots pine ●. As you descend, the presence of oak trees and the noise of traffic heralds the end of the walk. Soon there are roofs below and then a fence. The path zigzags down to the fence to reach the outward path. Turn right to return to the road. ●

Linn of Quoich

Start	Linn of Quoich, at the end of the road which passes Linn of Dee and Mar Lodge
Distance	3 miles (4.75km)
Approximate time	2 hours
Parking	At start
Refreshments	None
Ordnance Survey maps	Landranger 43 (Braemar & Blair Atholl), Explorer 404 (Braemar, Tomintoul, Glen Avon)

The long drive (or cycle ride) via the Linn of Dee and Mar Lodge to reach the starting point of this short route will provide nearly as much enjoyment as the walk itself. However, the walk should not be underestimated. It passes the cataracts and swirling pools of the Punch Bowl to follow the Quoich Water upstream through countryside which becomes increasingly wild. The path is narrow in places as it clings to the steep braeside. After crossing a remote bridge the return is on a Land Rover track which is left at a point near the bridge over the Punch Bowl which you cross to return through the woods.

Like the Linn of Dee to the west, which you will have passed on the way to the start of this route, the Linn of Quoich is a delightful spot to linger or set out a picnic. 'Linn' is the Gaelic word for 'pool', but the Quoich Water is actually comparatively shallow at the parking place by Allanaquoich – a boarded-up cottage with a red roof.

■ Walk upstream past the cottage into woodland. It is as well to heed the notice which warns of steep and slippery slopes. There is another abandoned cottage opposite the bridge ● just below the Punch Bowl, a large swirlpool which has recently been damaged. However, a spectacular series of potholes, ravines and cataracts remains intact, etched by Quoich Water over millennia. The water has a very distinctive azure colour as it rushes over the smooth rock.

Do not cross the bridge but continue to climb through the trees with the burn to the left. The path gradually becomes rougher and *it is easy to stumble on tree roots and slip on wet rock so keep well away from the edge and keep a close watch on children.* The pine trees are magnificent and provide food and shelter for a thriving colony of red squirrels. The deciduous trees, mainly birches, bring a blaze of colour to the glen in autumn. Rocky sections with chasms and waterfalls alternate with more gentle, pastoral views.

At length the path reaches a

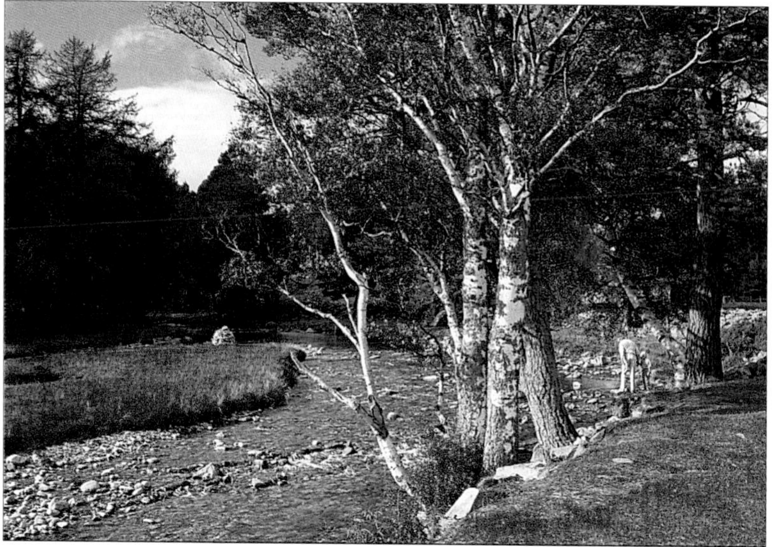

Linn of Quoich

comparatively broad valley and there are conifer plantings to the right. It rises to cling, sometimes not too successfully, to steep, heathery slopes. There are particularly fine views downstream with Morrone the dominant mountain behind. Just when you are despairing of ever finding the second footbridge you descend to cross a heather covered plain to arrive at the modern bridge which spans a narrow gorge ●.

There is a good Land Rover track on the other side of the Water of Quoich, providing much easier walking than any that has come before.

About 200 yds (183m) after the track leaves woodland into cleared land take the path to the left ● which descends gradually to reach the footbridge at the Punch Bowl ●. Cross the bridge and retrace your steps to the Linn of Quoich. ●

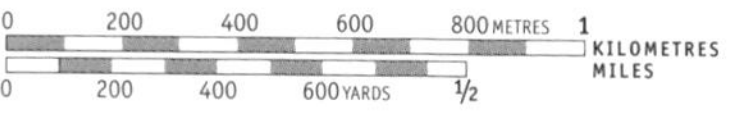

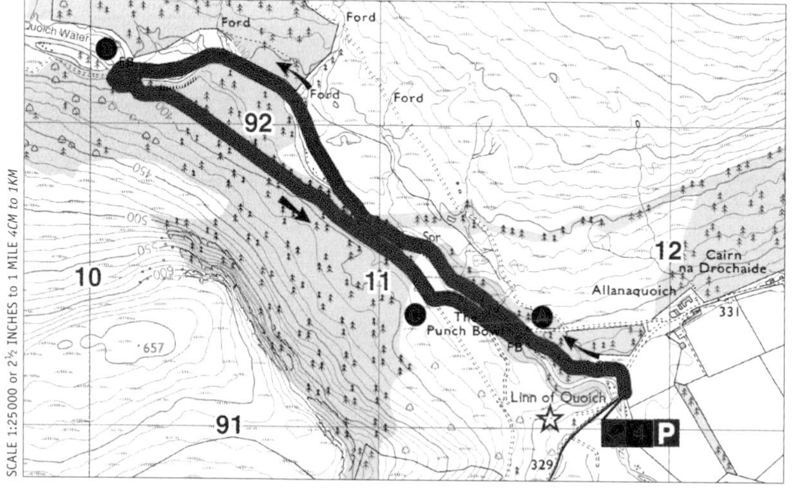

The Braes of Abernethy from Dorback Lodge

Start	At the end of the public road from Nethy Bridge
Distance	4½ miles (7.2km)
Approximate time	2½ hours
Parking	Limited parking in entrance to disused quarry just before the end of the road
Refreshments	None
Ordnance Survey maps	Landranger 36 (Grantown & Aviemore), Explorer 404 (Braemar, Tomintoul, Glen Avon)

Dorback Lodge is important as a centre where several long-distance hill tracks reach the civilisation of a metalled highway. However, it is unlikely that you will meet with anyone if you try this route which, on its outward leg, follows the northern side of the Dorback Burn into the romantic Braes of Abernethy. A little easy trail blazing is called for about two miles (3km) along this track when you leave it to follow the Allt nan Gamhuinn to reach the track on the other side of the valley. This gives glorious views northwards as it leads past a deserted farm to a ford over the Dorback Burn which might be difficult to cross after prolonged wet weather. It would be wise to check this first.

In the Braes of Abernethy

Note that the Braes of Abernethy should not be confused with the historic village in Perthshire or the famous Abernethy biscuit invented by a surgeon, John Abernethy (1764–1831). A 'brae' is a steep slope overlooking a river or burn. Here the Braes are the upper part of Abernethy Forest, the largest area of natural pine forest surviving in Britain.

Walk past the boarded-up lodge and the kennels, and then fork right **A** after the latter. Keep ahead when another track leaves to the right just before the second gate after the kennels. The track closely follows the course of the burn at first and can

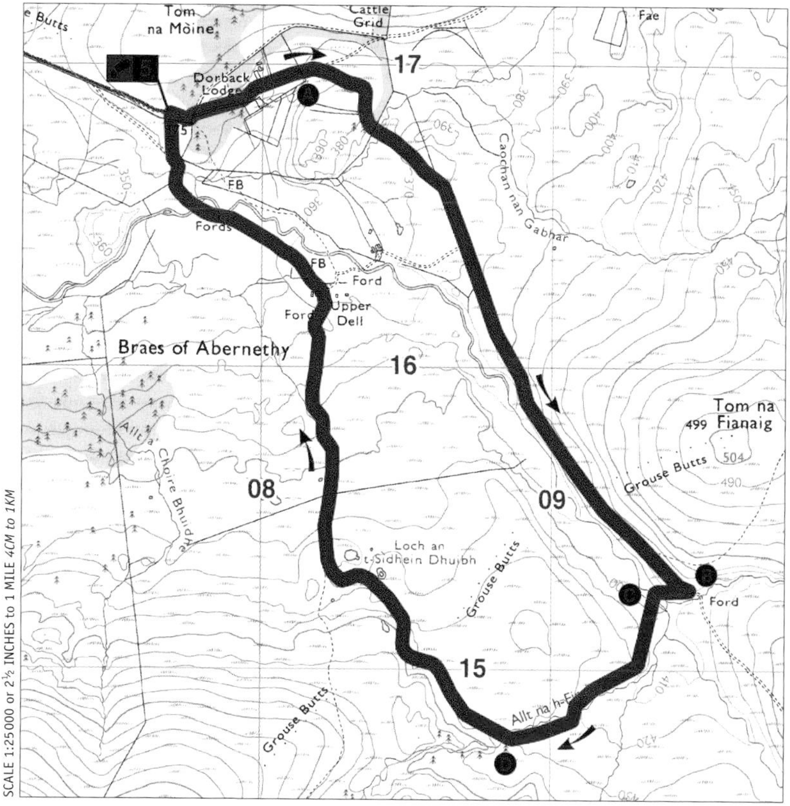

be seen climbing the hillside for miles ahead. Keep ahead again when another track leaves to the left heading up the slopes of Tom na Fianaig. The track eventually comes to a ford ●.

Instead of fording the burn here follow it down to reach the Dorback Burn by a solitary pine tree. Cross over the main stream ● and then follow the Allt na h-Eirghe upstream (south westwards). This part of the walk will be slow going, especially at times when the stream is flowing strongly and you are forced on to the heathery slopes above. If the water level is low progress will be easier and the stream will be crossed a number of times. You will probably be on the south side of the Allt na h-Eirghe when a group of pine trees comes into view. At this point ● the burn is forded by another track. Turn right on to this.

The track gives wonderful views over a famous tract of countryside, the Braes of Abernethy, as it winds its way back to Dorback. The braes are unusual in having generated sand dunes which rise above the banks of the river. These were initially caused by glacial deposits, later helped by the efforts of a thriving rabbit population. The way passes the ruined croft of Upper Dell and then crosses low marshland where the track has become very faint but leads to a ford which is crossed to a gate opposite. Go through this and turn right to follow a fence uphill to the starting point. ●

The Lily Loch and Loch an Eilein from Inverdruie

Start	Inverdruie
Distance	6 miles (9.7km)
Approximate time	3 hours
Parking	Public car park at Inverdruie
Refreshments	Einich restaurant, Rothimurchus Visitor Centre
Ordnance Survey maps	Landranger 36 (Grantown & Aviemore), Explorer 403 (Cairngorm & Aviemore)

Lochan Mor is better known to locals than to visitors as one of the scenic gems of the Cairngorms. Locals call it the Lily Loch and, fringed by pine trees and with its abundance of water lilies, it makes an enchanting picture in the summer. The walk makes a pleasant evening stroll (though you may need anti-midge precautions) and is an undemanding six-mile (9.7km) circuit with no taxing gradients. If you arrive at Loch an Eilein in the late afternoon you will see exhausted walkers who have completed the 20 miles (32km) of the Lairig Ghru from Deeside.

Long before the invention of Aviemore as a resort, Inverdruie was important as a centre of the timber industry. Pine trees from the Rothiemurchus Forest were brought to the village to be sawn into planks. Each spring the timber was heaped on to rafts made of logs and launched into the Spey to float down to the mouth of the river guided by two men, both wielding oars to manoeuvre the raft and prevent it from going aground.

Turn left out of the car park onto the road then, in a short distance turn left through a gap in the fence then left onto another road. Turn right and go through a kissing-gate on to a path which winds through the woods. The path emerges from the trees and crosses a stile and then a field to enter another wooded area where it divides A. Keep right here and continue for a short distance to merge with a wider path. This is a lovely part of the route through the ancient pines of the Rothiemurchus Forest.

Rothiemurchus means 'the grand plain of the fir trees' and it has been in the Grant family since 1574. The seat of this sept of the clan is at the Doune, the mansion about one mile (1.6km) south west of Inverdruie. Fittingly the emblem of Clan Grant is a sprig of Scots pine.

The Lily Loch, officially the Lochan Mor, comes into view suddenly B. First there is an enticing glimpse of brilliant blue water through the trees and then a little further on the lilies appear in all their glory (providing that you are actually here in the right season). It is an idyllic spot to linger on a hot day with the mountains blue in the distance.

Bear right and walk along the northern shore of the loch, passing a cottage to the right before coming to a road by Milton Cottage. Turn left and walk down the quiet road, but fork left ● at the entrance to the Loch an Eilein car park and turn left onto the public footpath to Braemar by the Lairig Ghru. Continue along the lochside for just over $^5/_8$ mile (1km) to cross a bridge at a junction of tracks ●. Follow the one signposted for Laraig Ghru – Glen Einich. At a fork in the road turn left following the cyclists sign. Go through the next crossing of paths to reach another crossroads where you turn left following the signposts to Coylumbridge. Keep on this track to go through a kissing-gate in a deer fence. Go through another gate and look for a red waymarker on the left in a couple of 100 feet. Turn left ● and go over a small footbridge then make your way uphill to reach the public road beside Whitewell. Go north along the road, crossing a cattle-grid and passing Upper Tullochgrue, where Lord Gordon found refuge for a time after the 1745 Jacobite uprising. At Blackpark another road joins from the left. Bear right and continue to follow the road back to Inverdruie. You will meet very little traffic on the way. ●

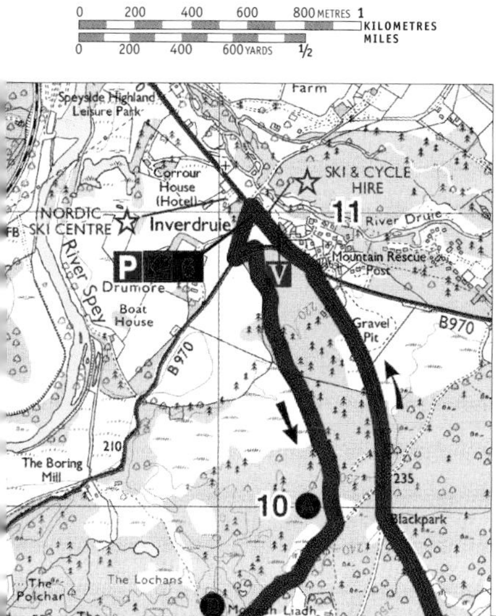

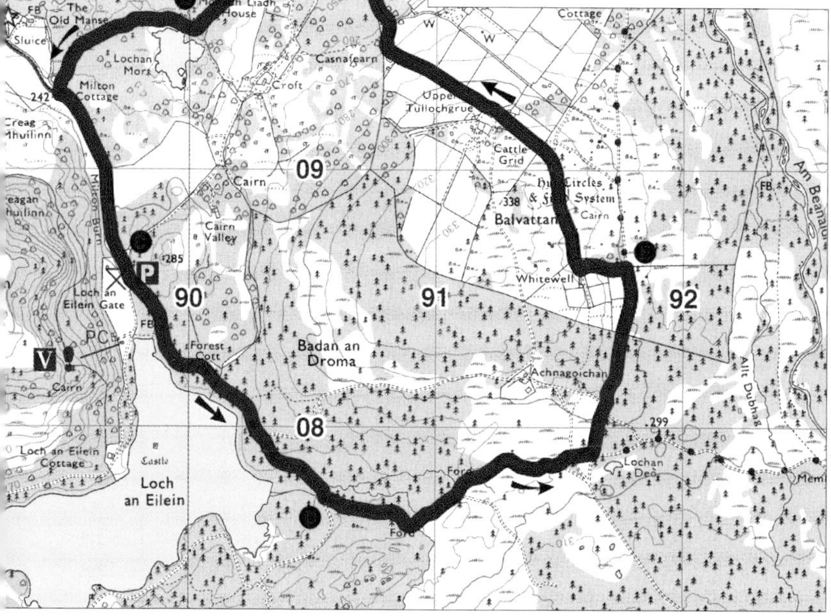

SCALE 1:29412 or about 2¼ INCHES to 1 MILE 3.4CM to 1KM

Creag Bheag and Loch Gynack from Kingussie

Start	Kingussie
Distance	4 miles (6.5km)
Approximate time	2½ hours
Parking	Kingussie central car park
Refreshments	Pubs and cafés in Kingussie
Ordnance Survey maps	Landranger 43 (Braemar & Blair Atholl), Explorer 402 (Badenoch & Upper Strathspey)

This walk, in the south west of the area where the River Spey separates the Cairngorms from the less spectacular Monadhliath range, takes you to the top of Creag Bheag, a fine rocky hill to the north of the village which provides wonderful views of the Cairngorm summits over the Spey valley. There are also views to the north beyond beautiful Loch Gynack, tree-fringed on its southern shore.

Kingussie, 'the head of the pinewood', was founded in the late 18th century by the Duke of Gordon on the opposite side of the Spey to Ruthven, the site of an earlier settlement where the Comyn of Badenoch had a castle and barracks were built by the government after the 1715 Jacobite Rising. In the 1745 Jacobite Uprising the barracks were successfully defended by Sergeant Molloy and 12 men against a besieging force of 300 Jacobites. The building was abandoned after Culloden and is now a romantic ruin well seen from the A9 trunk road. Like neighbouring Newtonmore, Kingussie has a notable shinty team and the game has been administered from here since 1993.

From the car park toilets follow the direction for Creag Beagh shown by the finger board. Cross a grassy area then turn right and up some steps to reach West Terrace. Turn right and where the road bends right by the Middle Terrace sign **A** keep ahead on a track finger-posted to Creag Beach. After 100 yds (91m) turn left through a metal gate and follow a well-waymarked path uphill through the woods. Pass through the remains of a deer fence and continue to follow the well defined path ignoring any turn offs. Eventually it will bend left to reach another waymarker by a junction. Keep straight ahead here. Just beyond the next waymarker the path becomes steep and stony. Climb up from here and through a gap in the deer fence **B** to reach a finger-post. Follow the direction arrow on this uphill towards Creag Beach.

The clear path that rises from here has a wall to the right at first as it climbs through heather to the top of Creag Bheag (1597ft/487m). After the end of the wall rest occasionally and enjoy the fine views back over Kingussie. The first cairn on the summit ridge proves to be one of a series (there are at least six). Continue north to see the view down to Loch Gynack from what is probably the summit cairn. The peak on the other side of the loch is Creag Dhubh which is also the battle cry of the Clan Macpherson. On the south west side of the hill is Cluny's Cave which served as a hideout both for the chief of the Clan, Ewen Macpherson, and the fugitive Bonnie Prince Charlie after the defeat at Culloden. Ewen evaded capture for eight years after this before eventually following the Prince to exile in France. After enjoying the view over the loch turn back to walk west, passing a lochan, on a path which later becomes indistinct.

Head to the left of the top of the loch (its south western end) as you descend over rough heather, avoiding rocky outcrops. Blue hares love these slopes and seem to delight in playing hide-and-seek with walkers. At the bottom join the path leading to the shore of Loch Gynack. This proves to be a delightful part of the walk though it is boggy in places. At the east end of Loch Gynack pick up the waymarkers for the golf course circular walk and go through a gate into a wooded area.

At the end of this wooded area follow the waymarks skirting the ruined Croft of Toman an Sèomair then continue along a high bank. At a waymarker in a dip turn left, then right at the next marker and follow the path through woodland.

Another waymark indicates a left turn. This is followed by a narrow steep downhill section with a handrail. The path eases as you reach a burn. Continue to reach a footbridge over the burn, then keep on the path to reach a T-junction with a tarred lane. A finger-post here indicates a right turn to head to Kingussie. Follow this down through the beautiful glen. Go past white gates and then, opposite the first house (Tigh Mor) take a path which leads down to another footbridge across the Gynack Burn. This one is built over a gorge where the water flows over cascades and through swirl pools. Turn left on to the road on the other side and follow this down to the car park entrance just before the main road. ●

0 200 400 600 800 METRES 1 KILOMETRES
MILES
0 200 400 600 YARDS ½

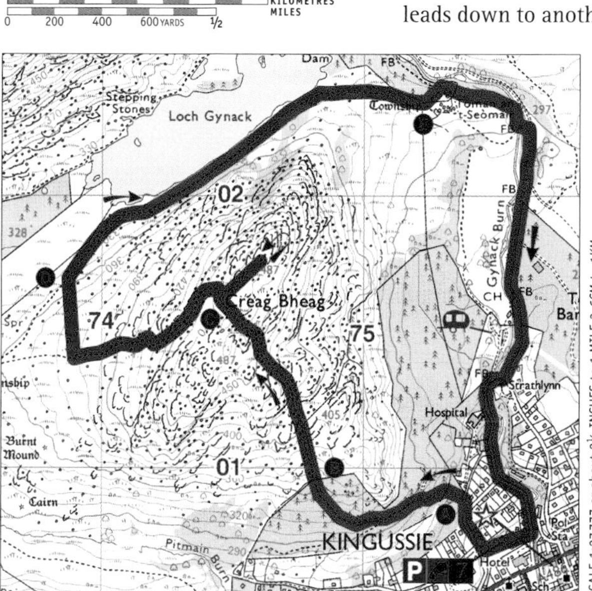

SCALE 1:27777 or about 2¼ INCHES to 1 MILE 3.6CM to 1KM

Glen Brown and Tom nam Marbh

Start	White Bridge, on A939 ½ mile (800m) east of Bridge of Brown and 3 miles (4.8km) north west of Tomintoul
Distance	4½ miles (7.25km)
Approximate time	2 hours
Parking	Layby at White Bridge
Refreshments	Tearoom at Bridge of Brown
Ordnance Survey maps	Explorers 404 (Braemar, Tomintoul, Glen Avon) and 419 (Grantown-on-Spey & Hills of Cromdale)

The Glenlivet Estate has excellent routes for walkers and provides leaflets and a descriptive booklet. This short walk takes you into the delightful countryside of Strath Avon and Glen Brown. Note that the route should not be walked between 6pm and 8am during the roe deer stalking season (end of April until 12 August, and the first three weeks of October). *Dogs must be kept on leads.*

■ Walk up the track on the edge of the plantation. There are power lines to the right while to the left, at the end of the planting, there is a fine view over Strath Avon. Go over the stile on the edge of the plantation and continue along the old sunken road. You are on a short length of the military road which was constructed in Strath Avon in 1754. This part of the Grampians, with its remote and inaccessible glens, was strongly Catholic and even after Culloden was regarded as a threat by the Hanoverians. A network of military roads was made so that troops could quickly reach any troublespot.

Leave this track when it swings to the left ● and follow a waymark which is pointing towards a pylon. The grassy path goes beneath power lines and climbs to a post where it swings left to descend to a damp area by a small burn. The path then climbs up again and runs along the side of the valley roughly ¼ mile (400m) from the main road. There are fine vistas from here as you enjoy level walking along the flank of the hill.

The path descends to cross a small birch wood and follows its lower edge with a fence to the left. You may well

Tom nam Marbh, an abandoned croft

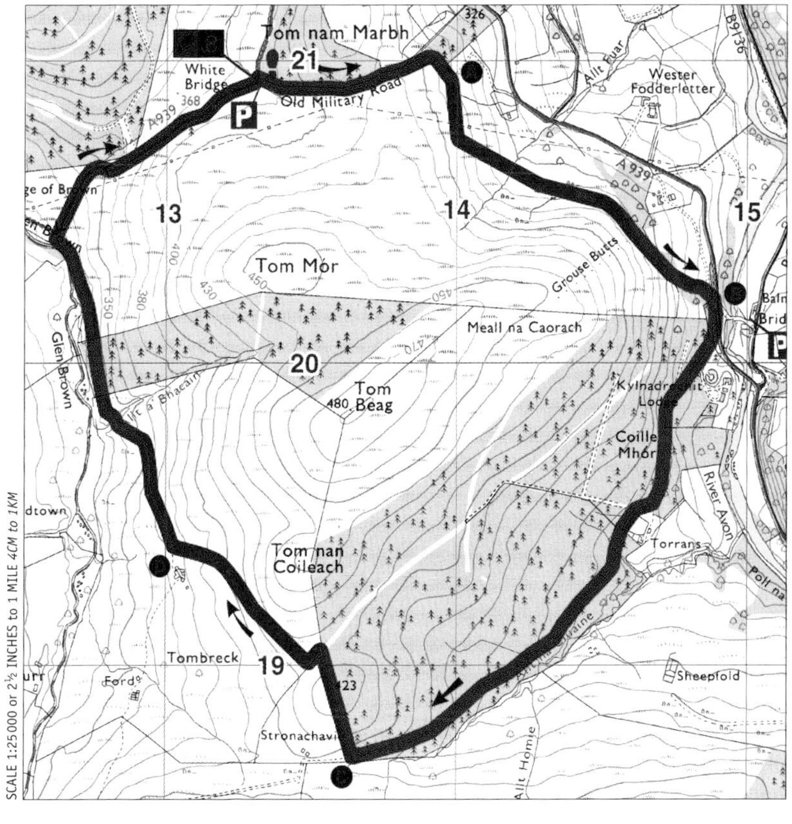

0 200 400 600 800 METRES 1 KILOMETRES
0 200 400 600 YARDS ½ MILES

see woodpeckers in the wood. Cross a stile into a pine wood which provides welcome shade on a hot day. The path descends gently to join a forest track near the Bridge of Avon, which is not visible from the walk ●. On reaching the forest track turn right.

Bear right when the track divides before a cottage and then bear left about 75 yds (68m) later. Pass through a gate after about 100 yds (91m). A long steady climb follows through the Kylnadrochit plantation to reach its western edge near Stronachavie, one of many local abandoned farms.

Cross the stile and turn right ● to follow the edge of the plantation uphill with the ruined farm to the left and a fence to the right. In early summer there are large multi-coloured violets on the hillside here. After the summit the path drops down to a fence and an old gate. Bear left here away from the forest, enjoying grand views to the left up Glen Brown, and follow another fence for a short way before passing through it at a gateway. The way then drops to reach another ruined croft, Tombreck. One of the crofts in the glen hereabouts flourished for a time, managing to support a family of 14.

Here you join a muddy track ● and this descends to reach the edge of a plantation just above the Burn of Brown. The track takes you to the main road just above the Bridge of Brown. Turn right and climb up the main road to return to the starting point at White Bridge. ●

The Five Bridges Walk, Ballater

Start	Ballater
Distance	5½ miles (8.75km)
Approximate time	3 hours
Parking	Ballater Station Square or behind Glen Muick church
Refreshments	Station restaurant in Ballater
Ordnance Survey maps	Landranger 44 (Ballater & Glen Clova), Explorers 388 (Lochnagar, Glen Muick & Glen Clova) and 405 (Aboyne, Alford & Strathdon)

There are no taxing gradients on this low level walk from Ballater which twice crosses the River Dee. The enchanting lochan hidden in the woods above the town is a beauty spot that locals prefer to keep secret. Later the walk runs through Dalliefour Wood where the forest drive provides shade in the summer or shelter if the weather is unkind. The last section of the route, above the River Dee, is especially glorious in autumn.

Ballater cannot claim to be an ancient town since its origins lie in the development of mineral springs at nearby Pananich in the 1790s. However, Queen Victoria's purchase of the Balmoral estate gave real impetus to its growth and the splendid station opposite the town hall was built in memory of Prince Albert. The station saw many regal passengers before its closure as branch lines became uneconomic.

The first of the bridges crossed is the Royal Bridge which spans the Dee on the south east side of the town. This was opened by Queen Victoria in 1885 to replace a wooden bridge built in 1834. This in turn superseded a stone bridge built by Telford which only lasted for 20 years. All this is testament to the power of the River Dee and to the skill of the designer and builders of the existing bridge.

■ After crossing the bridge cross the road to a finger-post. Ignore the waymarked path on your left and turn right to head uphill through the trees on a narrow track. Turn right to reach the memorial to Sir Alan Russell Mackenzie, laird of Glenmuick, who died in 1906. Return to the track and pass to the left of the monument. Keep an eye open for a green track branching off to the right and follow it to discover a beautiful lochan Ⓐ, restored by the Prince's Trust in memory of a local minister.

Retrace your steps for about 20 yds (18m) from the shore of the lochan and then turn left on a grassy path which takes you to the drive leading to the House of Glenmuick. Turn right here but then fork left off the drive almost immediately to descend to the road where you bear left, following the river.

The second of the bridges to be crossed is the little bridge across the Brackley Burn before the more impressive Bridge of Muick where the road up Glen Muick leaves to the left. The cairn here commemorates an occasion on September 16, 1899 when Queen Victoria attended a presentation of colours to the First Batallion of the Gordon Highlanders just before they embarked for South Africa. Many of the men who marched past her died in the campaign, including their commanding officer, Colonel Dowman. A straight length of road follows, which heads towards the ruin of Knock Castle, a stronghold built in the 16th century by the Huntly Gordons. About ½ mile (800m) down this road there is a house on the right and just past it a blue waymarker by the roadside indicates a right turn onto a sandy track

Take this sandy track **B** into Dalliefour Wood. It provides very pleasant, level walking and you will soon pass Dallyfour Cottage which has a particularly beautiful garden. The track runs straight and true through woodland for one mile (1.6km) or so before reaching the graceful, white painted suspension bridge over the Dee by Polhollick Cottage. Cross the bridge **C** and follow the track up to the main road (A93).

Cross the road and turn right. After 50 yds (46m) there is a gate on the left. Go through this and then turn

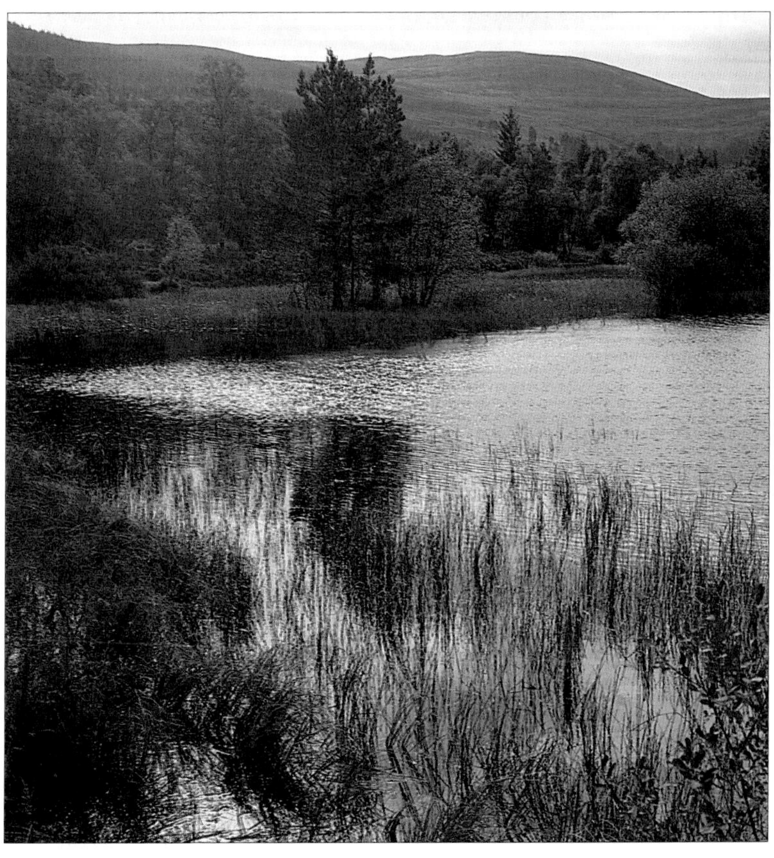

The lovely lochan in the forest

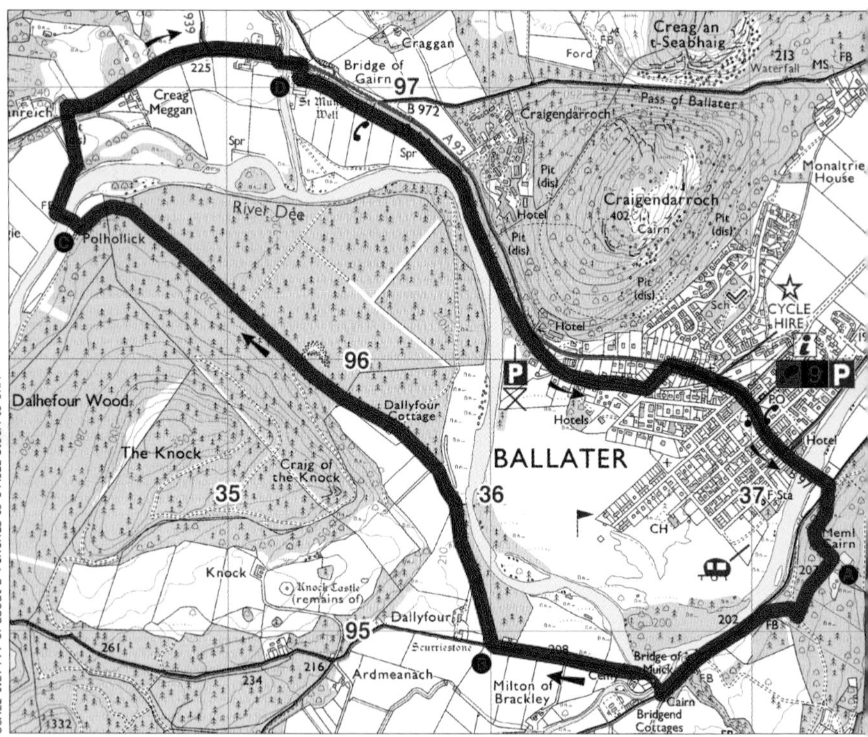

0	200	400	600	800 METRES	1 KILOMETRES
0	200	400	600 YARDS	½	MILES

right on to a path by a blue waymarker. It climbs up above the road and passes through encroaching bushes of broom. They provide an attractive foreground for pictures in the early summer. Follow the path until it descends to go through a gate and cross the Tomintoul road. Go through another gate and continue on the footpath until it joins the road at Bridge of Gairn ●.

This is the last of the five bridges and it takes the road over the River Gairn which has its source on the eastern slopes of Beinn a' Bhuird. St Mungo's Well, on the east bank of the Gairn, is dedicated to the memory of the 6th-century saint who founded Glasgow cathedral. He is also known as Kentigern and a church bears his name further down Deeside at Tulloch. Cross the road and take the path across the bridge. Then turn first right into the driveway of Bridgend of Gairn Farm and then immediately left onto a narrow path marked by an old white waymarker. This footpath gradually drops down to join a track after about 200 yds (183m). This makes a beautiful finale to the walk as it runs through woodland with the river flowing swiftly below. Old milestones by the track testify to its once having been the main road. There is a choice of paths, higher or lower, as you near Ballater; the lower passes through a picnic area before both paths meet again at the end of Old Line Road. When this road reaches the drive to the Balgonie Hotel keep ahead on the path which runs parallel to the Braemar road. However, you will eventually have to turn left into Invercauld Road to reach the main road by the Auld Kirk Hotel where you turn right to reach the town centre. ●

Glen Feshie

Start	At the end of the public road on the west side of Glen Feshie, just after it crosses Allt Chomhraig
Distance	6½ miles (10.5km)
Approximate time	3 hours
Parking	At start
Refreshments	None
Ordnance Survey maps	Landrangers 35 (Kingussie & Monadhliath Mountains), 36 (Grantown & Aviemore) and 43 (Braemar & Blair Atholl), Explorer 403 (Cairngorm & Aviemore)

You really need a mountain bike to get the best out of Glen Feshie; the long approach road to Carnachuin Lodge is closed to vehicles. At least you are unlikely to be troubled by traffic as you walk along this road through the forest. It leads to a footbridge over the river and a climb to one of the Cairngorms' most attractive waterfalls, hidden in lovely woodland on the side of the glen. Then you walk down to the river and follow it to cross the bridge again and return by the forest road.

Leave your car before the track goes off to Tolvah on the left and walk along the road. You soon reach a locked barrier as the road enters the forest. Pass this and continue on the road following yellow waymarkers. Ignore a turning to the right ● signposted to Drumguich and Kingussie. Keep ahead here following the sign to Braemar (26 miles, 42km).

Suddenly the road emerges from the trees and a grand view of the glen opens up. The waterfall can be seen in the woods on the other side of the valley. Cross a cattle-grid by the cottage at Stonetoper then veer left at the next passing place onto a rough path and follow it to the footbridge across the River Feshie ●.

Walk diagonally across the large field to steps over the deer fence which are directly opposite the derelict cottage on the riverbank (Achleum). On the other side of the fence follow the path which zigzags

The waterfall without a name

uphill following the course of the burn to the left. Just before the bottom of the waterfall cross another deer fence by a very rickety stile. The waterfall C is an idyllic spot set amongst pine trees. It seems strange that such a place has never been given a name. It will have taken you about an hour to get here.

Follow the path on the south side of the falls to the top, where the waters fan out, to be gathered again by a gorge a little lower down. Continue on by the stream until you find a suitable crossing point. You should come to a plank bridge which is covered and almost concealed by vegetation. Turn left on to the path on the north bank of the stream which joins with a track D coming down from Coire Arcain. Descend on this rocky track and pass to the left of the cottage (Achlean), crossing another path going to the waterfall. Head for the river on a narrow path. This fans out in several directions but keep straight ahead. Ford a burn then turn left at the river to follow it southwards. The footbridge over the stream from the waterfall E has disappeared so you may have to detour away from the river in order to cross it and so reach the derelict riverbank cottage. After this the way back to the footbridge B is straightforward close to the rushing waters of the Feshie.

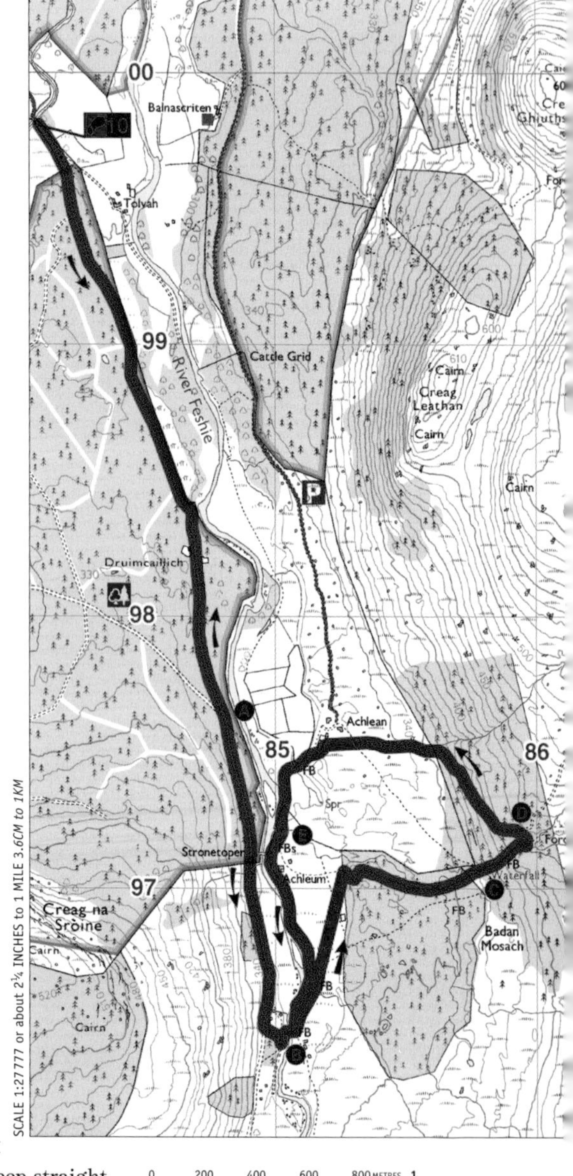

As you return along the forest road note the remains of a suspension bridge which once spanned the river opposite Stronetoper. Walking on the smooth and level surface again is pleasant and the scent of the pine trees fragrant, so the way back, if not exciting, is far from tedious. ●

Woodland and riverside from Grantown-on-Spey

Start	Burnfield, Grantown-on-Spey
Distance	7 miles (11.25km)
Approximate time	3 hours
Parking	Burnfield car park, Grantown-on-Spey
Refreshments	Pubs and cafés in Grantown-on-Spey
Ordnance Survey maps	Landranger 36 (Grantown & Aviemore), Explorer 419 (Grantown-on-Spey & Hills of Cromdale)

This is a walk which divides itself neatly into two: the outward part is through pleasant woodland leading to the River Spey and the homeward half follows the banks of the famous salmon river. There are no severe gradients on this walk and the paths should be dry unless the river is high after prolonged rain.

Burnfield car park is to the east of Grantown's main street; that is to the right as you begin to leave the town centre heading north on the A939, Nairn road.

Turn right from the car park and left at the end of the road. At the next junction turn right into Golf Course Road. Follow the track across the golf course and go through a gate into pine woods. The track is well-waymarked with the yellow waymarkers of the Speyside Way and red and blue markers of a forest walk.

The River Spey near Grantown

When the path divides by a seat bear left following the Speyside Way. There is a lovely mixture of trees – tall pines with rowans and birches. At the next junction bear left still on the Speyside Way and with the red waymarkers of a forest walk. Hills can be seen ahead through the trees as the track reaches another junction with a thoughtfully sited seat.

Turn right here still following the red markers and the Speyside Way. The path heads downhill to reach a fence beside a stream with open ground beyond. As the path starts to climb there is a junction on the right where the red path turns off. Keep ahead on the Speyside Way (A) and head uphill into a conifer plantation. After this the way is through a planting of conifers, curving down to another gate and meeting a track coming from the right. Bear left here to reach an iron gate, a cattle-grid, and a bridge over a burn. Turn right at a junction (B) to go through a gap

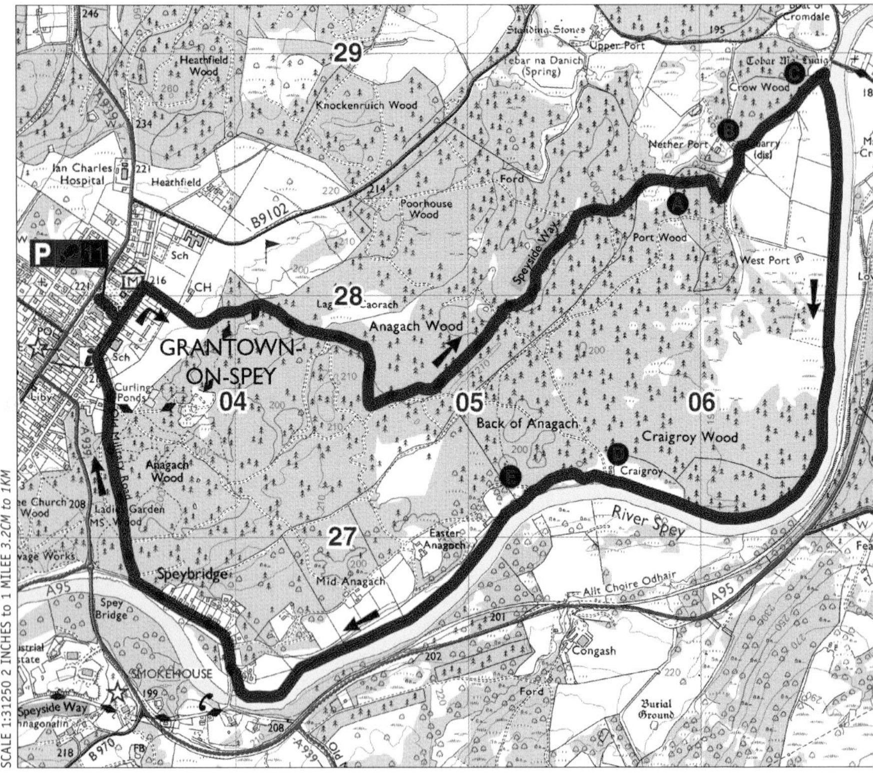

stile and follow a path which meanders beside the river to eventually merge onto a farm track just before Cromdale suspension bridge. Turn right here C. The open views and farmland contrast with what has gone before. Herons share the fishing with anglers and there is a vast population of mallard.

After about 20 minutes you will come to a fishermen's hut and enter woodland with the river making a tight curve below. Almost too soon the track comes out of the woodland. There is a pleasant seat to pause at where the track becomes a path rising up the riverbank to Craigroy D. Keep to the main track which goes through scrubby birch wood and juniper. About ¼ mile (400m) from Craigroy the electricity line crosses the track which is close to the river. As it swings to the right E take a narrow footpath on the left and head downhill through woodland towards the river.

The riverside path passes some of Scotland's best salmon beats and provides excellent walking, often on grass, to reach the Old Bridge at Speybridge. Walk up through the village and after the last house look for a yellow waymarker opposite a small car park. Turn right here, into Anagach Woods and follow the wide drive that is part of General Wade's road into Grantown and now part of the Speyside Way. The golf course is to the right before Wade's road reaches South Street opposite the fire station. Turn right and pass the primary school before taking the first turn left back to Burnfield car park. ●

Creag a Chalamain and Castle Hill

Start	Allt Mor car park
Distance	8½ miles (13km)
Approximate time	4½ hours
Parking	At start
Refreshments	None
Ordnance Survey maps	Landranger 36 (Grantown & Aviemore), Explorer 403 (Cairngorm & Aviemore)

The approach walk is on excellent paths, either newly constructed or restored and drained. The two hills are pathless, mostly over short heather and stones with thankfully short sections of longer heather at lower levels. The walk passes through beautiful Scots pine woodland, ending on forest roads. The high section is not recommended in mist, though a short cut is detailed below should inclement weather strike.

From the Allt Mor car park head off in a south-easterly direction indicated by a yellow marker post. Almost immediately cross a narrow timber footbridge over the Allt Mor. (The footbridge can be seen from the car park.) After crossing the footbridge turn right, this is the Allt Mor Trail.

Follow the Trail, taking care where it crosses the road, until point A is reached. Here another path joins from the road above. Turn right, crossing the Allt Mor on a long footbridge, known as Utsi's Bridge. Take note here of the natural erosion taking place as the Allt Mor carves its way through the glacial deposits, or 'till'. The path zigzags steeply up the far side of the gorge. Just before the top rim of the gorge take a left turn for the path leading to the Chalamain Gap. The Gap comes into view as higher ground is reached. To the left are superb views into the Northern Corries of the Cairngorm Mountains.

At B the burns are easily forded thanks to stepping stones. Here the narrower right-hand path can be used to cut out the hills in case of inclement weather, going straight to point D. However, assuming conditions permit, keep left and head straight up the steady climb towards the Chalamain Gap. The path is narrower now but still good.

At C, as the Chalamain Gap is approached, cross the small burn below the path on the right near a small pool, and before the ground on the right becomes too steep. The start of the climb to Creag Chalamain is steep and in deep heather but the gradient soon lessens and the heather soon becomes stunted. Keep going straight up and you are bound to reach the rocky summit. The views

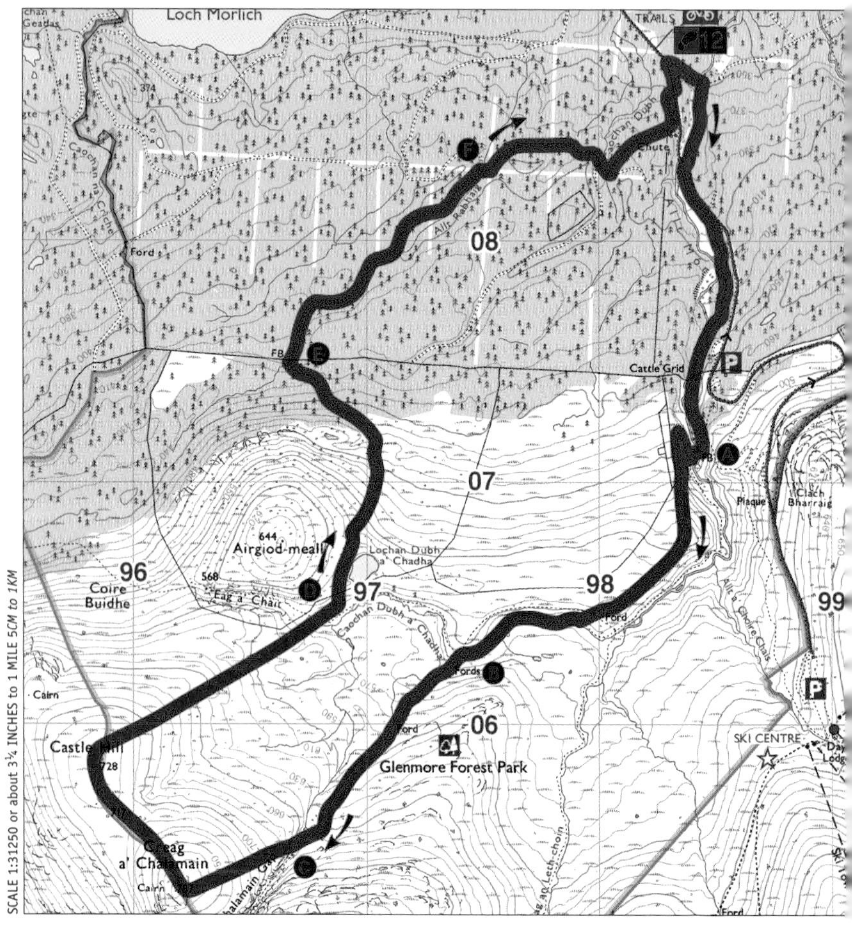

0 200 400 600 800 METRES 1 KILOMETRES
0 200 400 600 YARDS ½ MILES

from this, the highest point of the walk, are magnificent, especially those into the Lairig Ghru with Braeriach beyond.

Our route lies north-westwards to the small cairn on Castle Hill. Turn right at this cairn and descend aiming for Lochan Dubh a Chadha. The final section down to the path at the east end of the Eag a Chait (Cat's Gap) is rough going underfoot.

Locate the deer fence at **D** and follow the track east for a few yards until a left turn is seen heading up towards the fence. Reach the fence and follow it for 150 yds (137m) to a stile. Cross the stile and follow the path to the left of Lochan Dubh a Chadha, and over a low col. The path drops down and enters the forest, winding as it does through some beautiful Scots' Pines.

At **E** cross the burn below Utsi's Hut onto the end of a forest road. Follow this to the right to stay next to the burn.

At **F** turn right at the junction of the forest roads. In 500 yds (457m) turn left at the next junction of forest roads and follow this to the main road. Just before the junction with the road turn left onto a blue waymarked cycle path. It's a short distance from here to the car park which is concealed in the trees. Look out for the signpost then leave the path to cross the road to the car park. ●

Carrbridge and General Wade's Road

Start	Carrbridge
Distance	7½ miles (12km)
Approximate time	3½ hours
Parking	Carrbridge car park
Refreshments	Pubs and cafés in Carrbridge
Ordnance Survey maps	Landranger 36 (Grantown & Aviemore), Explorer 403 (Cairngorm & Aviemore)

This is an enjoyable low level ramble through forest and moor and on paths along meadows and riverbanks. The highlight of the walk is General Wade's Road which is followed as far as Sluggan Bridge, a memorable beauty spot. From here a path leads back to Carrbridge, never far from the River Dulnain. Note that after heavy rain there may be difficulty in fording Allt Lorgy.

From the car park on the Aviemore road (B9153) turn right and walk down the road as far as the post office. Turn left here, just before the bridge, on to Station Road. The remains of the famous packhorse bridge, built in 1717, can be seen on the right. It was badly damaged in the disastrous flood of August 1829.

Pass the road to the station on the left and go beneath the railway and then the main road (A9). Turn off the

The old bridge, Carrbridge

road to the left A after passing land awaiting development and immediately before a timber yard. Keep the timber yard to the right and follow the rough road to reach a metal gate at the edge of a wood. Go through the gate and continue along a forest road. After some distance in pine forest the road goes through an area of birch and then heathland. This gives good views northwards and cars can be seen climbing the Slochd summit.

Just before this road bends to the left look for a green track B branching off to the right and turn onto it. Keep following it, go through a wooden gate and continue. The track passes beneath power lines and carries on through a ghostly patch of forest with crimson fungi and trees spangled with lichen. Turn right at a T-junction on to General Wade's Road C.

The sandy track leads down to a ford, which is the crossing point of the Allt Lorgy D. The crossing itself may call for the removal of boots and socks and the rolling up of trousers. The track climbs and at the top of the hill there is a crossroads. Keep ahead – fine views open up both in front and to the right. The stumps of felled Scots' pines look as though they could well have been standing when General Wade constructed the road during the 18th century. Bear right when a track leaves to the left. After this the road strikes northwards in a straight line and passes beneath power lines. After about one mile (1.6km) it crosses a road.

General Wade's Road is now more picturesque as it winds down through pines and birches. It may be very wet at times. At a junction turn left and continue downhill. The highlight of the walk comes as the way opens up and reaches East Sluggan, lush grassland shaded by mature trees. Cross the wonderful packhorse bridge and then turn right E to pass a ruined croft. There is a fine view of the bridge as another path is joined which runs through bracken along the edge of a wood. Climb a high deer gate. On the other side the path is through heather rather than bracken.

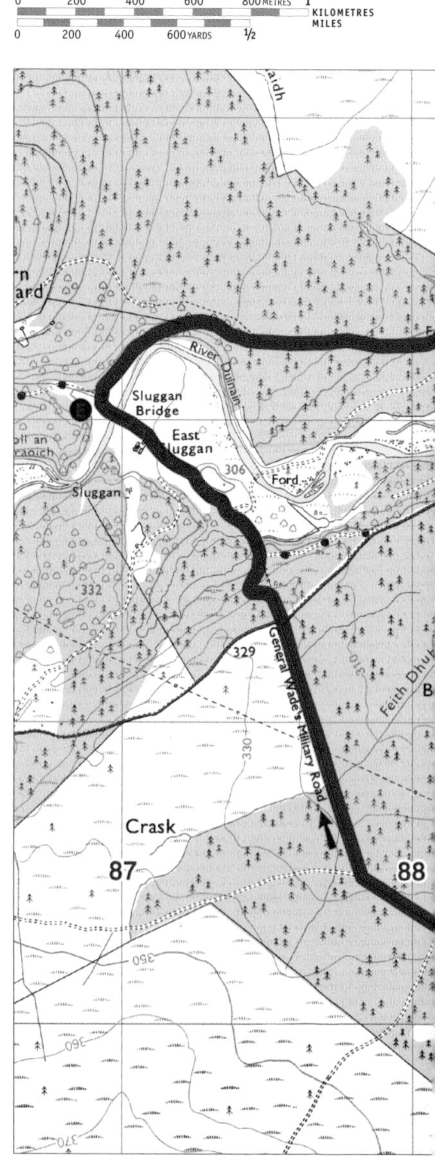

There are good views of the River Dulnain. The path joins a track of red earth which passes a redundant stile and then descends to a deer fence and a burn. After fording the burn the path follows the course of the river closely and the new bridge carrying the A9 is seen ahead. Bear slightly to the left away from the river on to a causeway which takes you to a footbridge by a house named Lynphail.

After crossing the bridge *(its boards are slippery when wet)* join the track and walk down it to cross the A9 and pass beneath the railway. Continue along the road from the railway bridge, passing some wooden buildings on the right, then turn right on a downhill path leading to a suspension bridge. Turn left when the path meets a track leading to trekking stables. Turn left when the track meets Station Road and follow this back to the main road. Turn right to the car park.

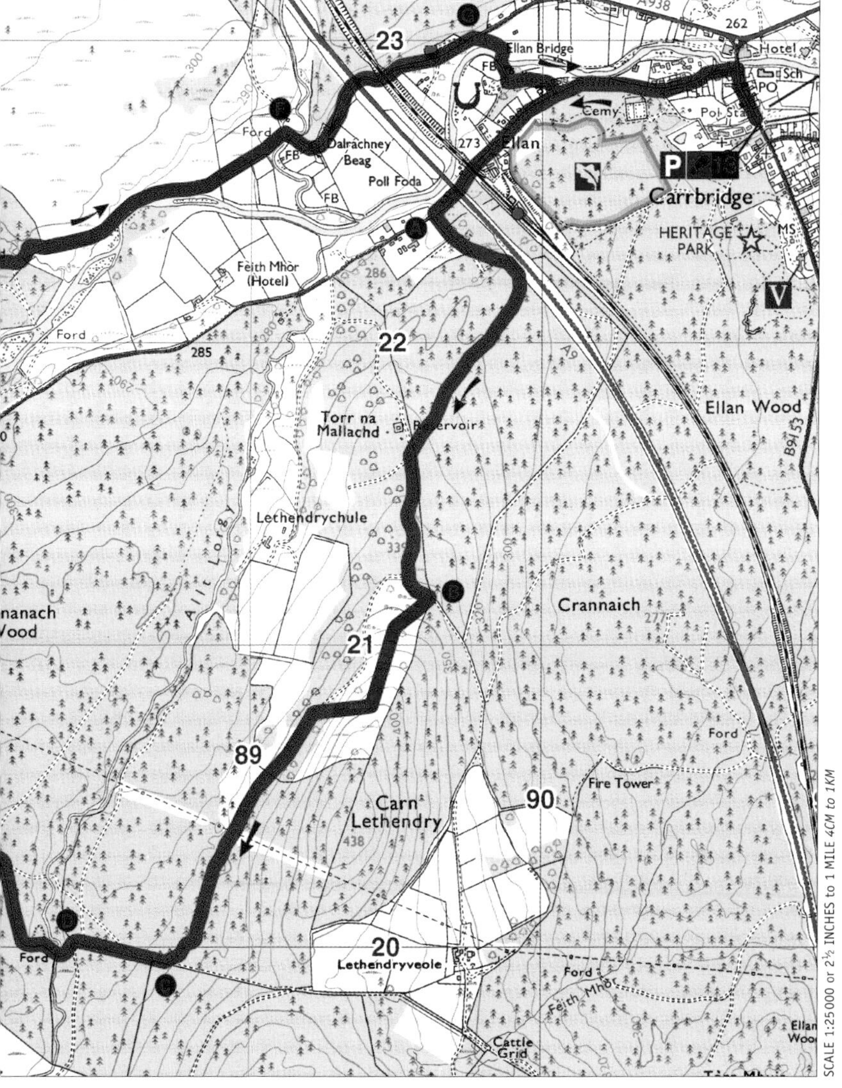

The Red Well from Newtonmore

Start	Newtonmore
Distance	6 miles (9.7km)
Approximate time	3 hours
Parking	Public car parks near church in Glen Road (the one nearest the church is reserved for churchgoers on Sundays)
Refreshments	Pubs and cafés in Newtonmore
Ordnance Survey maps	Landranger 35 (Kingussie & Monadhliath Mountains), Explorer 402 (Badenoch & Upper Strathspey)

This is an exhilarating walk up to the lonely moorland of the Monadhliath Mountains which lie to the north of Newtonmore. It would be unwise to attempt this route in poor visibility since the outward path is very faint at the top before it swings east to meet the Land Rover track near the site of the Green Bothy, a landmark which has now vanished from the scene. However, the Red Well is still to be found a little farther up the track and its water is tasty and refreshing.

Note that you should not park in the upper car park on Glen Road (next to St Bride's church) on a Sunday.

Walk up the road past the church. After about ½ mile (800m), just before a cattle-grid turn right **A** on a track going to Upper Knock. Bear left when the track divides near the top cottage. The rough track ends abruptly but the route continues on a sunken, grassy way which passes through a patch of birch scrub to come to a gate to the right of a planting of firs. The scene looks bleak ahead but it is well worth persevering. Look back at the fine view of Strath Spey with the Cairngorms beyond for reassurance.

This gate is a rare landmark

At the top of the conifer planting the way ahead is discernible as a banked,

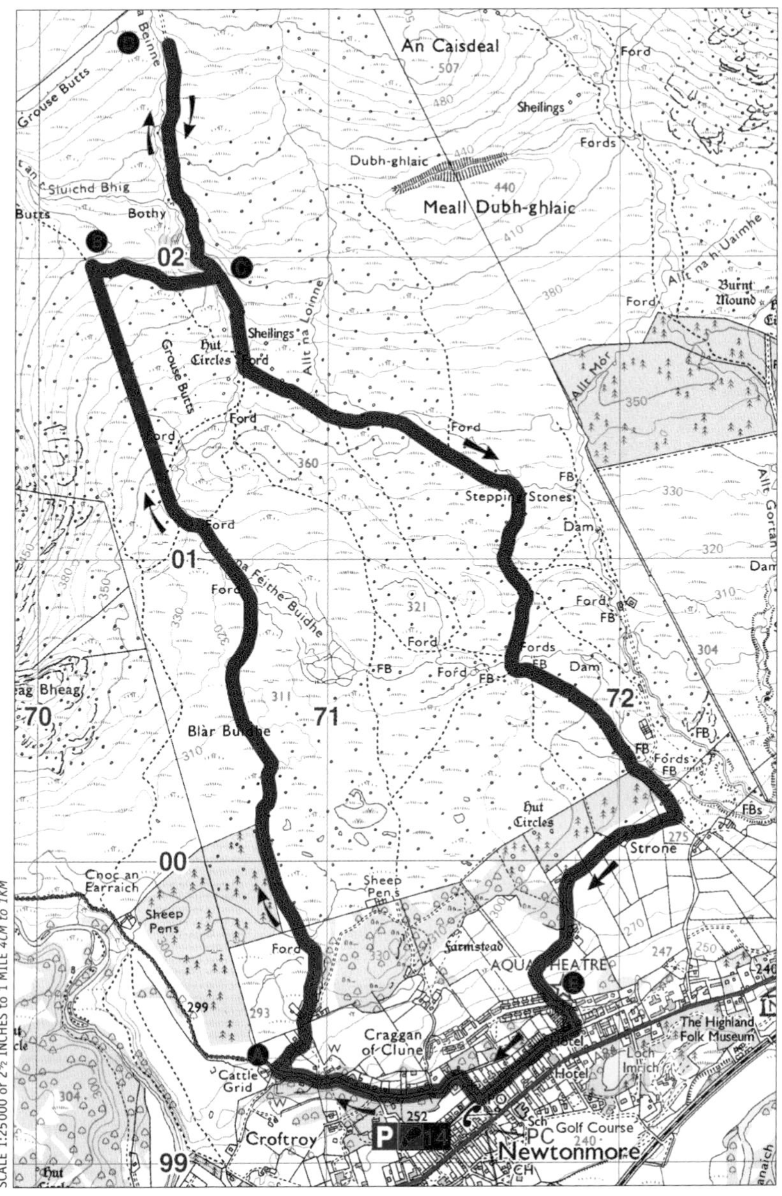

SCALE 1:25 000 or 2½ INCHES to 1 MILE 4CM to 1KM

0 200 400 600 800 METRES 1 KILOMETRES

0 200 400 600 YARDS ½ MILES

grassy path descending to a causeway of large boulders. Note that though the line of the path is not always clear on the ground, it follows the line of the conifer planting over wetland and then uphill, heading just to the west of north. There is no obvious path through the bog which you reach near a fence – hopefully you will be able to see a gate in the fence and reach it without wet socks.

After the gate a faint path crosses a stream and climbs with the stream to the right. The path becomes very faint but a boulder on the skyline, which at first might be mistaken for a deer, provides a useful landmark.

Look back occasionally to enjoy the view and make sure that you are still following the line of the planting.

The boulder turns out to be a triangular stone. Turn right (eastwards) about 50 yds (46m) before reaching the top of the ridge **B**. Alternatively you may prefer to climb to the stone and look back to see the path which heads eastwards. It comes just at the point where heather gives way to grass. The path has sunk between banks of heather. It descends to round the shoulder of a hill and a track comes into view on the left with a stream running beside it. Make for the track and turn left on reaching it **C**.

The Red Well

Climb up the track past the site of the Green Bothy, once a landmark which was visible from many points in Newtonmore. All that remains is the rusty corrugated iron of its roof.

Climb briskly for another seven minutes and you will see the unmistakable colour of the Red Well's water to the left **D**, on the far side of the burn. It is as rusty as the roof of the bothy. A rock with an arrow and the initials JD stands on the right-hand side of the track at this point. Another rock by the spring itself bears more initials and the date 1869. There is usually a mug on the stone to catch the red water which is surprisingly palatable.

Return down the track from this point passing the site of the bothy. It is very pleasant walking in this direction with a good view facing you and often grass underfoot. A tall cairn to the right appears to have been made of the stones of grouse butts. The white buildings to the left look something like a swimming pool but are waterworks. The path comes out at a road by the remains of an old barn. Turn right here and follow the road over a cattle-grid before coming to another road at a telephone box **E**. Turn left on to Clune Terrace and then right to pass the Highland Pottery and return to the starting point. ●

Glen Lui and Derry Lodge

Start	Linn of Dee car park, 6 miles (9.7km) west of Braemar
Distance	7 miles (11.25km)
Approximate time	3 hours
Parking	Car park at Linn of Dee
Refreshments	None
Ordnance Survey maps	Landranger 43 (Braemar & Blair Atholl), Explorers 387 (Glen Shee & Braemar) and 403 (Cairngorm & Aviemore)

The track up Glen Lui is the most popular approach to the southern Cairngorms. This walk explores the glen as far as Derry Lodge, an abandoned hunting lodge set in one of the most beautiful corners of the Grampian hills. The route lies on the Mar Lodge Estate, which was acquired by the National Trust for Scotland in 1995. Red deer culling takes place from 1 July to 15 February, and during this period walkers are asked not to deviate from recognised hill tracks, of which this walk is one. A short section of path towards the end of the walk can occasionally be slippery and potentially hazardous, and is not suitable for young children.

From the car park at Linn of Dee take the footpath signposted to Glen Lui. Head uphill on a forest path then downhill and across some duckboards. Eventually reach a Land Rover track and turn left ●. (There are actually two paths, one from each half of the car park, which converge after about 50 yds [45m]). Turn left here, and take note of the East Grampian Deer Management Group information board. One of the aims of the National Trust for Scotland is the regeneration of natural woodland, which involves culling the huge herds of red deer that roam the estate. Many of the Scots' pines in Glen Lui are 150 to 200-years-old, but there is very little new growth outside the fenced enclosures because the deer eat the saplings.

After walking approximately ¾ mile (1.2km) from the gate you cross the Black Bridge over the Lui Water ● and turn left. From the bridge there is a fine view up the glen towards Derry Cairngorm (the conical summit on the right) and Ben Macdui, which at 4296ft (1309m) is the second highest mountain in Britain. The glen here is broad and green, with grassy pastures by the river where herds of red deer are sometimes seen. The valley was once farmed, but the crofters were forcibly evicted in 1726 and, although some people later returned, by 1840 the farms had been completely abandoned. Today all that remains is the occasional ruckle of stones by the roadside marking the

Mature Scots' pines in lower Glen Lui

ruins of dykes and cottages.

A further two miles (3.2km) of easy walking brings you to Derry Lodge. Originally built as a hunting lodge for the estate, it was leased in the 1950s to the Cairngorm Club who used it as a base for expeditions into the mountains. It now lies unused, looking rather forlorn with its boarded-up windows. Just past the lodge is a wooden shed containing mountain rescue equipment and an emergency public telephone.

On a sunny day, the edge of the woods at the confluence of the Derry and Luibeg burns makes a fine picnic spot Ⓒ. Here you can recline on a lush bed of grass beside the stream and admire the view towards Luibeg Cottage. Glen Luibeg is the gateway to the Lairig Ghru, probably the finest mountain pass in Britain, leading to Rothiemurchus and Aviemore. Off to your right (north) is Glen Derry, the start of another cross-country walking route over the Lairig an Laoigh to the Fords of Avon, and then by Bynack More or Strath Nethy to Loch Morlich, or down Glen Avon to Tomintoul.

Begin the return leg of the walk by following the path along the left bank of the Lui Water, which passes the remains of Bob Scott's Bothy, before rejoining the Land Rover track. (The bothy, destroyed by fire in December 2003, commemorated the Mar Lodge gamekeeper who lived in Luibeg Cottage in the 1950s, and was a great friend to climbers and walkers.)

Retrace the outward route as far as the gate at Ⓐ, but keep straight on along the track. About 250 yds (228m) farther on, where the forestry fence on the left comes to an end, a side path leads to the Lui Water at a series of beautiful pools and waterfalls. A short distance upstream, beside the largest fall, is an old salmon ladder. *(NB: The path up to the salmon ladder is occasionally steep and slippery, and is not suitable for young children. Take great care.)* Return to the track and continue down the glen to the tarmac road. Turn right and follow the road for ¼ mile (400m) back to the car park. ●

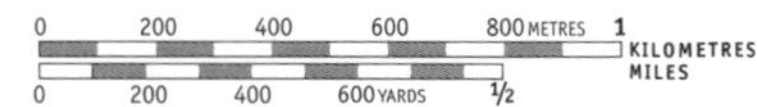

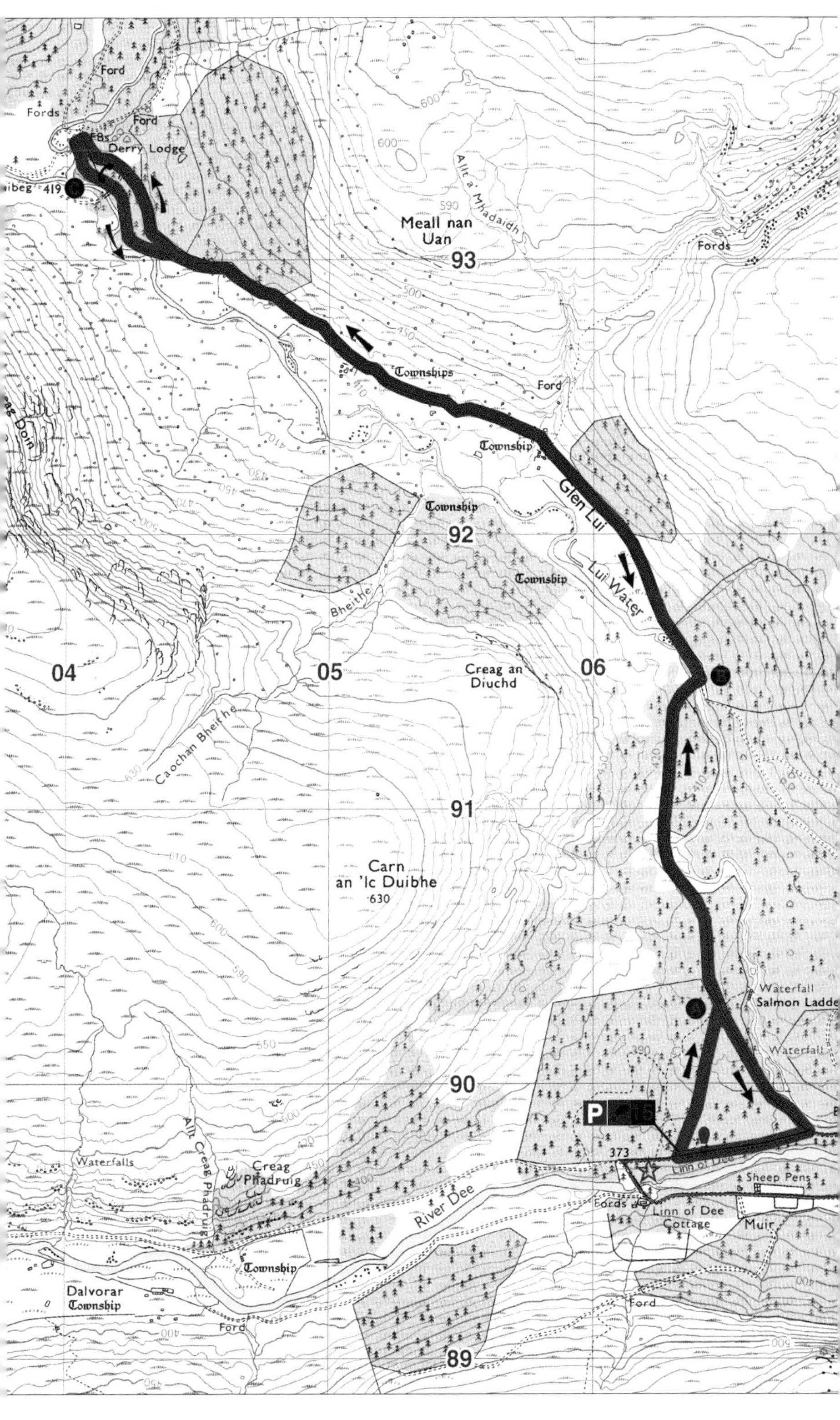

Ford
Fords
Ford
FBs
Derry Lodge
419
Meall nan
Uan
Allt a' Mhadaidh
Fords
Townships
Ford
Township
Glen Lui
Township
Township
Lui Water
Bheithe
04
05
Creag an
Diuchd
06
Caochan Bheithe
91
Carn
an 'Ic Duibhe
630
Waterfall
Salmon Ladder
Waterfall
90
P
373
Linn of Dee
Sheep Pens
Waterfalls
Creag
Phadruig
Allt Creag Phadruig
River Dee
Fords
Linn of Dee
Cottage
Muir
Township
Dalvorar
Township
Ford
Ford
89
93
92

Carn Daimh from Glenlivet

Start	Tomnavoulin
Distance	6½ miles (10.5km)
Approximate time	3½ hours
Parking	Clash Wood car park. This is reached via the byway which leaves the main road (B9008) to the left as you drive northwards out of the village
Refreshments	None
Ordnance Survey maps	Explorer 419 (Grantown-on-Spey & Hills of Cromdale)

This is another of the excellent walks maintained and waymarked by the Glenlivet Estate. It takes you through remote farmland and forest before joining the Speyside Way and then climbing to the summit of Carn Daimh which, at 1866ft (570m), is a splendid viewpoint. However, the best moment in the walk comes as a finale, when the path drops into Glenlivet and you are faced with a wonderful scene of high, heather covered hills on the far side of the verdant glen.

A Walk up the forest track from the car park for about 200 yds (183m) before leaving it to the left to follow a 'Walk 5' waymark ('Walk 9' continues ahead). The footpath leaves the forest and skirts pastures with woodland to the right. Go over a stile at the end of the plantation and through the gate facing you **B** on to the farm track which leads to Westertown.

Immediately after this point another track, to Easter Corrie, leaves to the right. Ignore this and keep on the lower track to Westertown, perhaps pausing occasionally to enjoy the fine view back to Glenlivet.

After Westertown cross the Allt a' Choire by a plank bridge just upstream from the ford. After passing through a belt of trees the track crosses the Slough Burn (a tributary of Allt a' Choire) and then climbs steeply to swing left towards Craighead, an abandoned farm. Leave the track here **C** by keeping ahead to climb through fields with the ruin to the left.

The steady climb southwards eventually brings you to a track leading to a plantation. Look back to take in the fine view to the north, dominated by Ben Rinnes (2759ft/840m) whose beautiful conical outline gives it an importance to the scene out of scale to its height. There are more fine hills to the east beyond Glenlivet as the track enters the forest. Soon after reaching level ground you come to a signpost bearing the Speyside Way symbol. Turn right here **D** to join this route following the sign to Ballindalloch.

The path twists and turns through the forest, falling and rising, before it reaches a gate which gives on to open country. Follow the long track by the

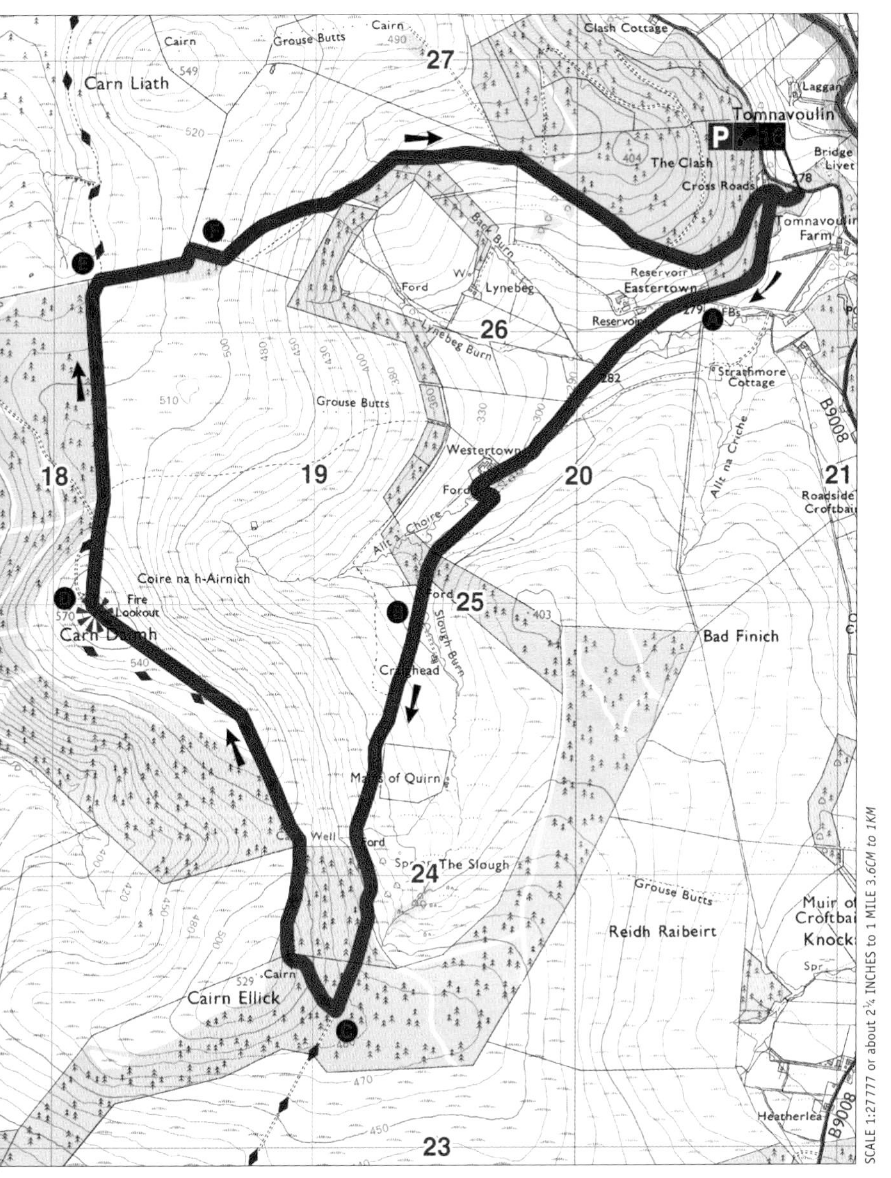

side of the plantation up to the summit of Carn Daimh ● which is at 1866ft (570m) and affords a glorious panorama of the countryside surrounding Glenlivet. There is an indicator identifying the variety of landmarks which you should be able to see from here on a good day.

From Carn Daimh take the track due north which follows the fence and drops down to a plantation. Here a path leaves to the right to Tomnavoulin via Westertown which could serve as a short cut if time is short. Continue northwards to the bottom corner of the plantation ● where the path turns to the east. After 100 yds (91m) the Speyside Way leaves to the left but our route keeps ahead, following the fence. The way through the heather gets easier to follow as you climb.

The path turns left at a corner of the fence by a lone, stunted Scots pine. After 100 yds (91m) turn right to follow an older fence down towards Tomnavoulin. Before reaching a plantation the way swings left to go through an old gateway F and then strikes across the heather towards the left end of the plantation. The path along the western side of the plantation goes past a firebreak and then crosses a field to join a forestry track. This track gives wonderful views to Corryhabbie Hill, the highest of the rolling hills beyond Glenlivet. There are conifers to the left and beautiful birches to the right before you re-enter Clash Wood and soon return to the starting point. ●

Corryhabbie Hill and Glenlivet

A Walk around Loch Muick

Start	Spittal of Glen Muick
Distance	7½ miles (12km)
Approximate time	3½ hours
Parking	Car park at the end of the road to Spittal of Glen Muick
Refreshments	None
Ordnance Survey maps	Landranger 44 (Ballater & Glen Clova), Explorer 388 (Lochnagar, Glen Muick & Glen Clova)

There is little need for skills in wayfaring or map reading on this walk – once on the shore of the loch it is just a matter of walking with Loch Muick to the left. Its name may derive from the Gaelic and mean 'the loch of the swine', or alternatively it may come from the Norse 'myrkr' from which we get the word 'murky'. Queen Victoria preferred to think of it as 'the lake of sorrow' even though she and Prince Albert spent many happy days here.

Although the Scottish word 'spittal' is derived from 'hospital' it would be a mistake to think that sick people were once brought to the Spittal of Glen Muick to be healed. The hospice which was once situated here provided shelter for travellers who were trying to cross the dangerous mountain passes. Later it was used by drovers and it actually survived until the mid-19th century when railways began to provide speedier ways of transporting cattle.

A Follow the track from the car park to the visitor centre where there is an exhibition about the 6,350 acre (2570 ha) reserve. This part of the Glen Muick estate was amongst the land added to the Balmoral Estate by King George VI between 1947 and 1951. The reserve area was established in 1970 when the Estate set up the visitor centre and employed the first countryside ranger. Beyond the visitor centre a signpost points ahead to the direct route to Lochnagar. Bear left to follow the sign to Loch Muick. Keep on towards the loch when a track leaves to the left. This is the Capel

Loch Muick

Mounth, the ancient way to Glen Clova used by smugglers and rustlers as well as by units of Bonnie Prince Charlie's army en route to their defeat at Culloden.

About a mile along the path from the visitor centre, and 300 yds (274m) before a clump of trees, turn right (A) on to a path going towards the north end of Loch Muick. This is a wide, well-made path which crosses a wooden bridge and passes a boathouse. After this it joins the main driveway (B) along the northern shore of the loch which goes to Glas-allt-Shiel. Queen Victoria built this lodge after the death of Prince Albert as 'my first widow's house, not built by him or hallowed by his memory' and it became one of her favourite haunts. The walking is easy on this smooth track and the steep, dark slopes on the far side of the loch are always dramatic and sometimes seem almost menacing. Byron roamed these hills as a boy and it is easy to understand how memories of such scenery inspired his poetry. He wrote a splendid piece on Lochnagar and compared the English countryside unfavourably with that of Scotland.

Just before reaching the woods surrounding Glas-allt-Shiel leave the drive to the right on to a path (C) which climbs to cross a wooden bridge. The pretty path passes into the woods above the lodge and crosses the Glas Allt, a more considerable burn. A pleasant but fairly energetic diversion here is to take the path which zigzags up the hill by the Glas Allt to the spectacular waterfall at the top. The way to the waterfall leaves just after the second bridge (D), where the main route around the loch follows the path around the top edge of the woods and then heads down to the lochside.

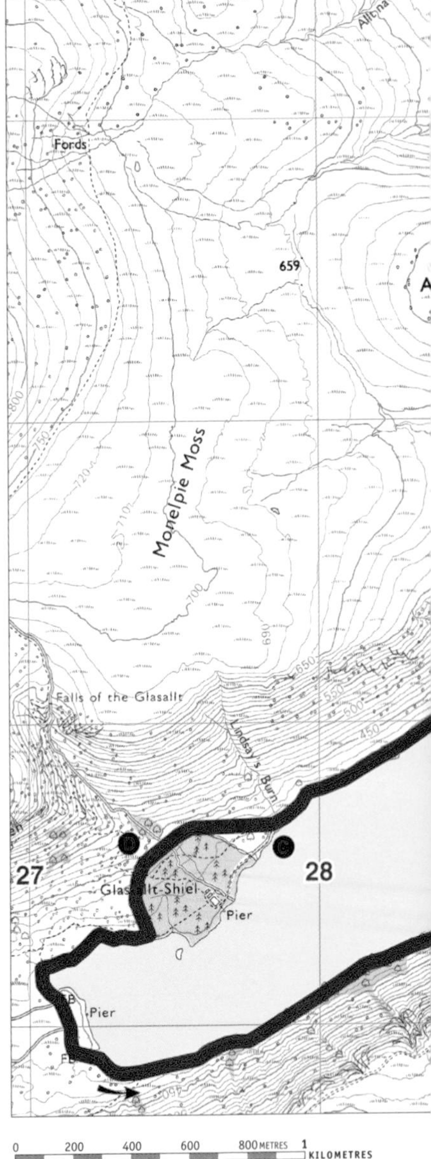

Keep to the path which is closest to the shore and runs around the western end of Loch Muick. A path to the right goes up the glen to Dubh Loch, another place of austere beauty which Queen Victoria often visited. It was during one of her excursions, which took in the Glas Allt waterfall and Dubh Loch, that she learned of

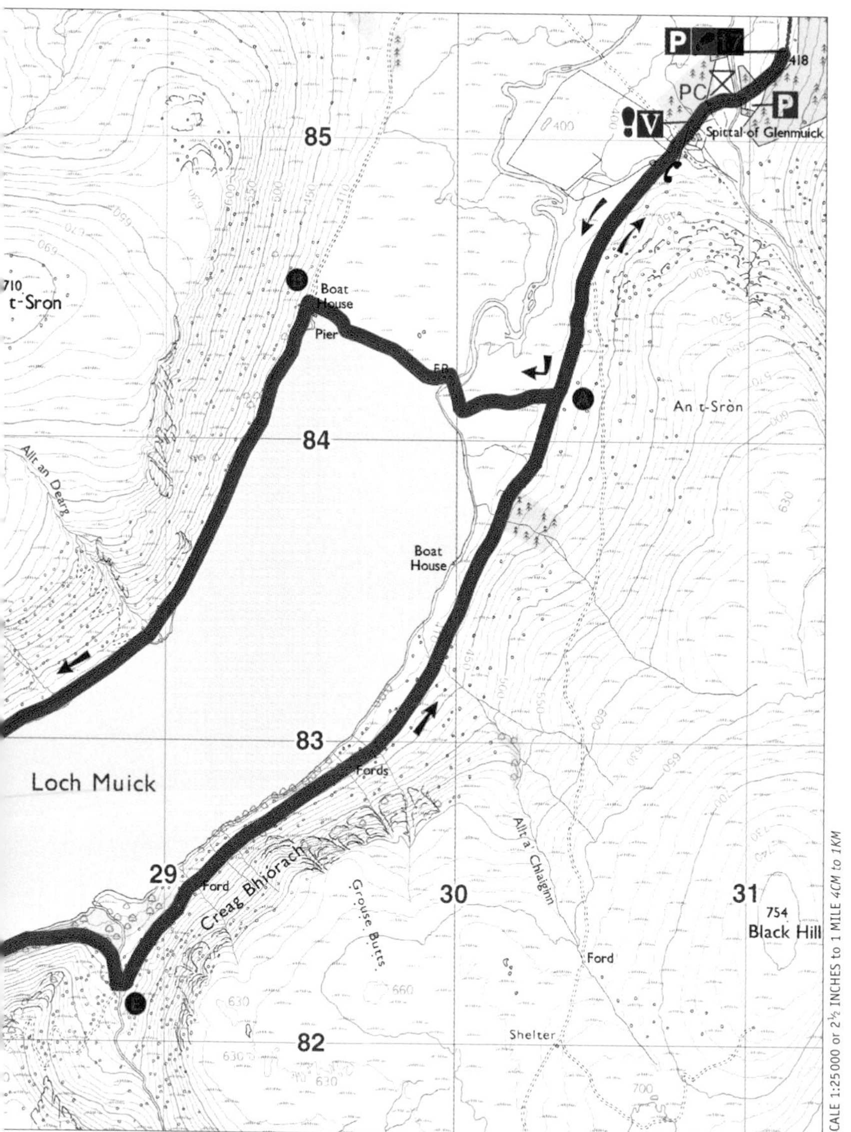

the death of the Duke of Wellington. This was in September 1852. There is a beach with golden sand which makes an ideal playground. This too was a spot loved by the old Queen and was frequently used as the venue for royal picnics.

The return leg of the walk is by a narrow path which clings to steep slopes clothed with birches, blaeberries and foxgloves. The birch trees are particularly beautiful as the path approaches the bridge over the Black Burn where it joins the track mentioned earlier coming from the Cairn Bannoch ridge E.

The final two miles or so by the side of the loch are comparatively unspectacular but the going is easy and the views ahead rewarding. After passing an isolated clump of trees the track leaves the lochside and soon returns to the visitor centre and the car park.

Eag a' Chait and Loch Morlich

Start	The bridge at the west end of Loch Morlich
Distance	7 miles (11.25km)
Approximate time	4½ hours
Parking	At start
Refreshments	None
Ordnance Survey maps	Landranger 36 (Grantown & Aviemore), Explorer 403 (Cairngorm & Aviemore)

The route provides a mixture of scenery with forestry plantings at first as the road gradually climbs to Rothiemurchus Lodge. This modern group of buildings is set in moorland dotted with clumps of old Scots' pines. The path then climbs to the rocky pass of Eag a' Chait, giving grand views to the Cairngorm summits. However, just below the top of the pass the route turns northwards to head back to Loch Morlich, at first through a wonderful area of ancient forest (where you stand a chance of meeting reindeer) and then through plantings. The return is along forestry tracks above the southern side of the loch, which is relatively unfrequented but just as beautiful as the more popular shores.

Cross the bridge and walk up the track towards Rothiemurchus Lodge. The track is initially close to the shore and soon divides. Keep ahead to Lochan nan Geadas which is reached after about 15 minutes. This delightful little stretch of water is a secluded paradise for wildlife. There are good views of the hills ahead including the conical Castle Hill which rises to the south of Eag a' Chait. When the track divides (A) take the left fork and head towards Rothiemurchus Lodge.

Unfortunately, the path shown on the map which leaves the track shortly after this junction has been lost so there is no alternative to following the track to the Lodge. The scenery changes at a cattle-grid where forestry plantings end. When you reach the Lodge walk through the complex, bearing to the right of the top building towards the helipad.

From here (B) the path is vague as it crosses boggy ground. Head east for the saddle between Airgiod-meall and Castle Hill. Having skirted a hillock topped with a handful of Scots' pines, the path crosses a final short stretch of boggy ground to a path climbing Coire Buidhe. The path becomes distinct as it rises above tree level and a wide view opens up to Loch Morlich. The steepest part of the climb comes when the deer fence is

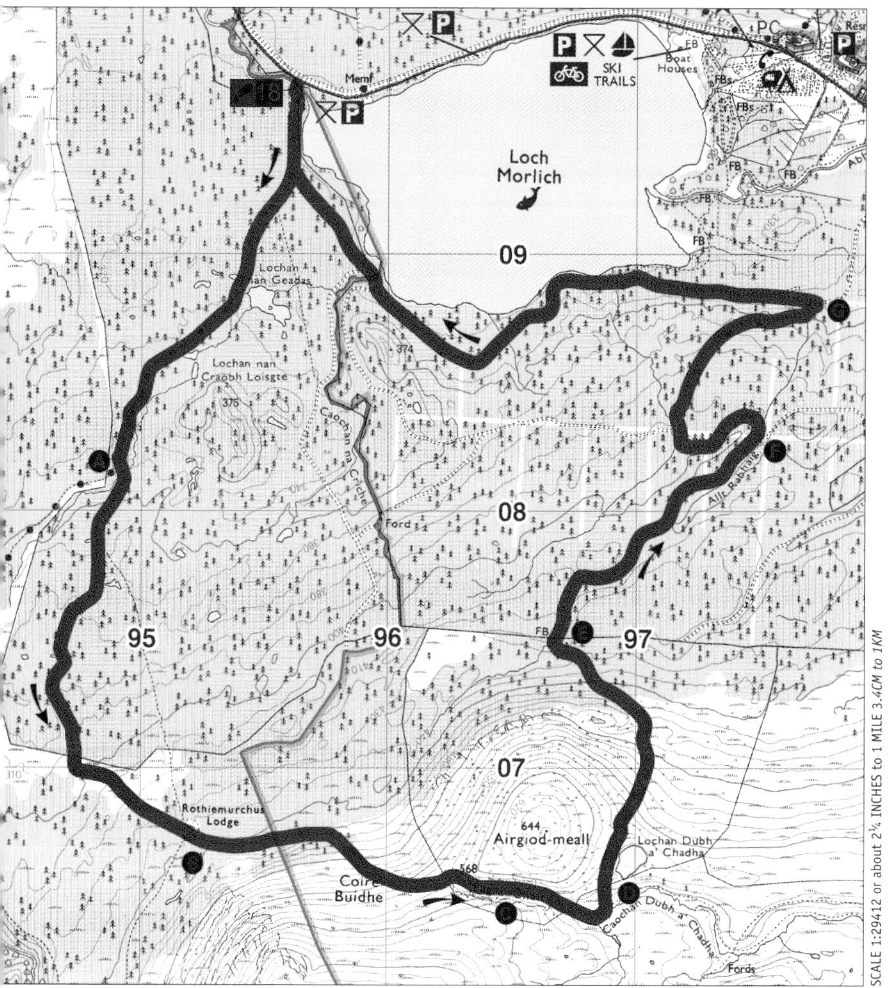

reached, but this section is brief and you are soon in Eag a' Chait C.

The pass is filled with scattered boulders but these end just beyond the summit. Shortly after the boulders end look for a path to the left D which climbs to the deer fence. Walk by the side of the deer fence for about 150 yds (137m) to find steps over it. The path then skirts Lochan Dubh a' Chadha. From here there is a spectacular view across the water to the summits, corries and plateau of the Cairngorm massif.

The path begins to descend with Loch Morlich ahead and the Kincardine Hills beyond. It is interesting to see Scots pine seedlings struggling to survive. This heads north to cross a dry valley and then descends through mature pines. It crosses a clearing with electricity poles and then comes to a forest hut locally known as Utsi's Hut after Mikel Utsi who re-introduced reindeer to the Cairngorms. On the other side of a lovely burn there is a gate giving on to a forest track E and by it a notice: '*Dangifer Tarundas* Beware the Bulls', this with a painting of a reindeer. This area, including the part you have just

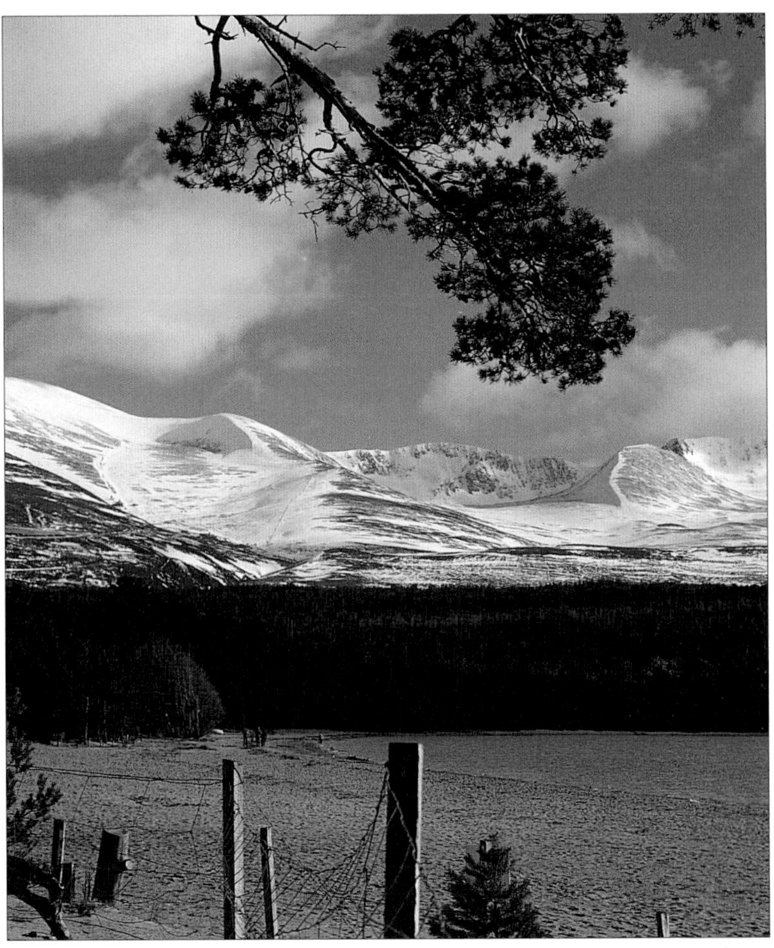

Loch Morlich

walked through is a reindeer enclosure. *Signs advise you to stick to the paths.* During May and June the deer are calving and you should do nothing that might disturb them. In September and October it is rutting season and some bulls can become aggressive. The sign advises that you enter at your own risk. However you should not encounter any problems if you stick to the paths. Further information can be obtained from the Reindeer Co Ltd on tel. 01479 861228.

The track follows the stream which was crossed earlier. When the track divides at F turn left and proceed to the next junction of forest roads, which is in about 500 yds (457m). Turn right here and continue for about ½ mile (800m) to yet another junction of forest roads.

Turn left on to a broad track G, this track leads along the southern shore of Loch Morlich.

The broad sandy track gives views of the loch at first but soon leaves it. You will still be following red-topped posts but bear right to leave them when they lead to the left. Cross a stile into the Rothiemurchus Estate and follow the good sandy path which gives views across the loch, with windsurfers providing colour and action. At a T-junction turn right to retrace your steps to the bridge at the start. ●

Loch an Eilein

Start	Coylum Bridge
Distance	8 miles (12.75km)
Approximate time	3 hours
Parking	Layby on south side of B970 just before campsite and bridge
Refreshments	The Einich restaurant Rothiemurchus Visitor Centre
Ordnance Survey maps	Landranger 36 (Grantown & Aviemore), Explorer 403 (Cairngorm & Aviemore)

The lack of any severe gradients on this walk will appeal to many and, although flat, the route has much to offer in the way of fine scenery. It starts by the Coylum Bridge campsite at the beginning of the Lairig Ghru, the long distance path which leads over the mountains to Braemar. This takes you to the Cairngorm Club footbridge where there is a choice of burnside picnic sites, some with sandy beaches. Then the way is westwards through ancient Scots' pines and past beautiful lochans to Loch an Eilein. Most people arrive at this popular beauty spot by car and do not venture as far as its western shores so you should be able to enjoy peaceful walking along the paths away from the car park. The return to Coylum Bridge is on estate roads and footpaths through more of the beautiful and fragrant Rothiemurchus pine forest.

The start of the Lairig Ghru is marked on the main road by a green signpost. The track passes the campsite and even here the character of the Rothiemurchus forest is apparent with its beautiful old Scots' pines. Keep a lookout for red squirrels on this walk: if you have a dog it will alert you to their presence in the boughs above, and you may see the remains of neatly nibbled pine cones. Pass Lairig Ghru Cottage on an excellent level path which follows the stream, 100 yds (91m) or so away from its bank. In about ½ mile (800m) bear left when the path divides **A**. The other path is signed to Glen Einich. After a stile over a wall

Beautiful Lochan Deò

the path crosses a burn and becomes narrow with banks of heather on each side. The sound of rushing water increases as you approach a gate and from here there is a view of the mountains ahead, with the notch that the Lairig Ghru passes through clearly visible. A short distance farther on a track leaves to the right Ⓑ but continue to the river and to the Cairngorm Club footbridge where, if you wish, you can explore a little further to find quiet picnic places by the river, often with sandy beaches which will appeal to youngsters.

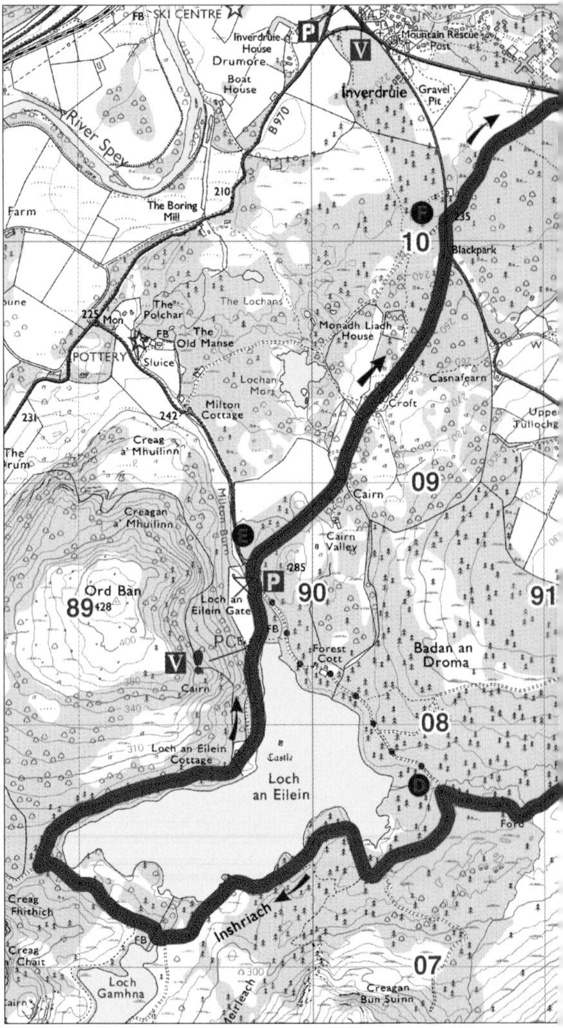

Return to Ⓑ and fork left following the sign to Loch an Eilein. The track crosses an attractive heather-covered heath scattered with Scots' pines. There is a fine view back from this enjoyable section of the walk. The lovely little Lochan Deò is on the left just before the path comes to a crossways Ⓒ. Keep ahead here and cross two sparkling burns by footbridges. Loch an Eilein comes into view soon after this in its woodland setting.

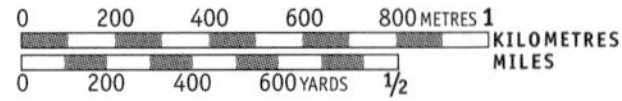

Turn left when you come to the T-junction Ⓓ above the eastern shore of the loch. *If you wish you can shorten the route by turning right here.* Pass a bench sited by a large stone and follow the path in a clockwise direction around the loch. Sometimes the path is close to the water, often it is at some distance. The loch seems to grow in size as you walk westwards. At the head of the loch there is a wooden bridge which gives a view of the neighbouring Loch Gamhna. Another in a series of well situated seats is nearby and a path goes off left round Kennapole Hill which is crowned by a memorial cairn to a Duchess of Bedford.

Within about 20 minutes you pass Loch an Eilein Cottage, where the loch is fringed with cherry trees, and immediately after this comes the castle itself. This was a stronghold of Alexander Stewart, Earl of Buchan, the bastard son of King Robert II, who was given the name of 'the Wolf of Badenoch' from the savagery of his bitter feud with the clergy which resulted in his being excommunicated. This was after he had put the town of Forres to the torch and burned down the cathedral at Elgin. He died in about 1405 and achieved an undeserved fame by being made the swash-buckling hero of a Victorian novel.

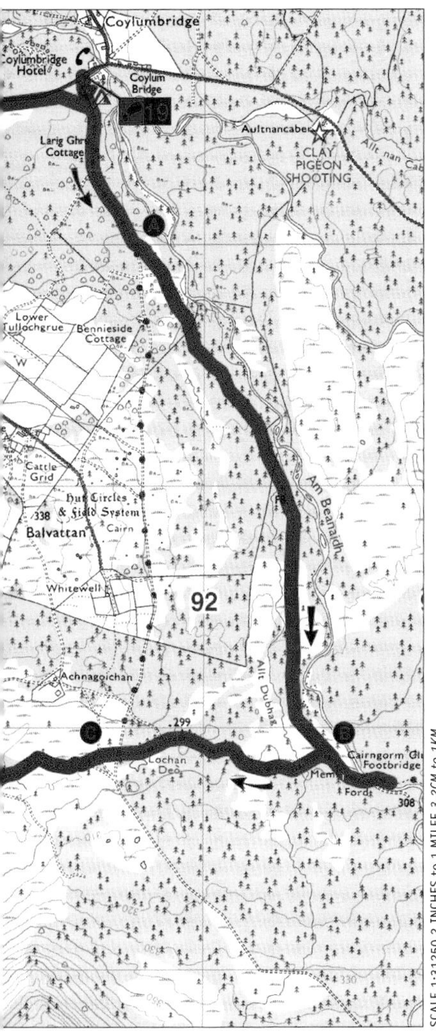

SCALE 1:31250 2 INCHES to 1 MILEE 3.2CM to 1KM

In 1690 the castle was besieged by a group of Jacobites retreating after their defeat at the Battle of Cromdale. The defence was led by a formidable lady, Dame Grizel Mor Grant, who was the widow of the fifth laird Grant and who supervised the casting of ammunition for her garrison. At this time the castle was connected to the shore by an easily defended zigzag causeway but this was lost when the level of the loch was raised in the 18th century. If you shout vigorously across the loch you may hear a unique triple echo as your voice is bounced to and fro from the crumbling walls of the castle to the tree-covered hillsides.

From the castle it is only a short step to the car park, a good place to be at about 6pm when weary walkers and mountain-bikers limp in from excursions over the Lairig Ghru. Pass the car park on the left then cross a bridge and turn right 100 yds (91m) beyond E on to a track with a notice which requests 'Estate vehicles only please'. There are times when you can catch a glimpse of Lochan Mor (better known as the 'Lily Loch') through trees to the left before passing cottages to the right and a big house, Monadh Liadh, to the left.

The very pleasant track joins a surfaced road at Blackpark. Keep straight on but within ¼ mile (400m) turn right F on to a footpath which crosses the road. This grassy path is an enjoyable finale to the walk as it leads through Scots' pines and divides opposite the entrance to Coylumbridge Resort Hotel. At this point take the right fork to continue walking parallel to the road and you will eventually reach the Lairig Ghru track by a gate. Turn left here to reach the B970 at Coylum Bridge and the layby from which you set off. ●

Fiacaill and Cairn Lochan

Start	Cairngorm chairlift car park
Distance	6½ miles (10.5km)
Approximate time	5 hours
Parking	Car park at the top of the Ski Road
Refreshments	Café and bar at chairlift
Ordnance Survey maps	Landranger 36 (Grantown & Aviemore), Explorer 403 (Cairngorm & Aviemore)

It would be foolish to pretend that the climb to the Cairngorm plateau via the Fiacaill ridge is an easy one. However, there is much satisfaction in climbing to the rim of Coire an t-Sneachda, and after reaching the midway point of the chairlift neither this, nor the ski tows and funicular, intrude on the scenery. The traverse of two of the most spectacular Cairngorm corries is exciting. However, this walk is not one to undertake in the mist as, not only would spectacular views be missed, but expert navigation would be required.

Walk up the path which passes to the left of the bottom chairlift station and then climb up the service road which leads to the midway station. This will take about 15 minutes and is the most tedious part of the ascent. Keep to the main path which passes beneath the cables just before the first disembarkation point. After the station the broad track climbs steeply and makes a sharp left hand bend. Look for the path to the right **A** which leaves the summit path here and is signposted to Fiacaill. A flight of stone steps takes the path up from the main track.

The climb is steep but enjoyable and much effort has been spent in keeping the path in good repair. Keep to the centre of the path to avoid damaging the delicate vegetation on either side. As you near the top the path becomes rather more diffuse and there are wonderful views from the narrowing buttress of Coire Cas to the left and the dark crags of Coire an t-Sneachda to the right. At last the large cairn **B** comes into view. It will have taken you about an hour to reach this from the car park.

Walk around the edge of Coire an t-Sneachda following the cairns. It is easy to think that the way might be less difficult if you took to less stony ground to the left. This would be a mistake: you would not only increase the distance but the stupendous views northwards, framed by crags and pinnacles, would be missed.

At the western side of Coire an t-Sneachda the well trodden path to Ben Macdui strikes southwards (to the left) **C**. Instead of taking this

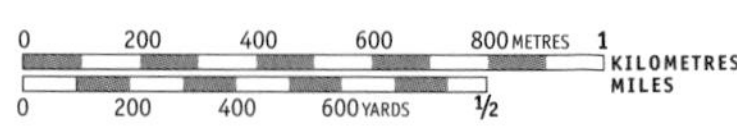

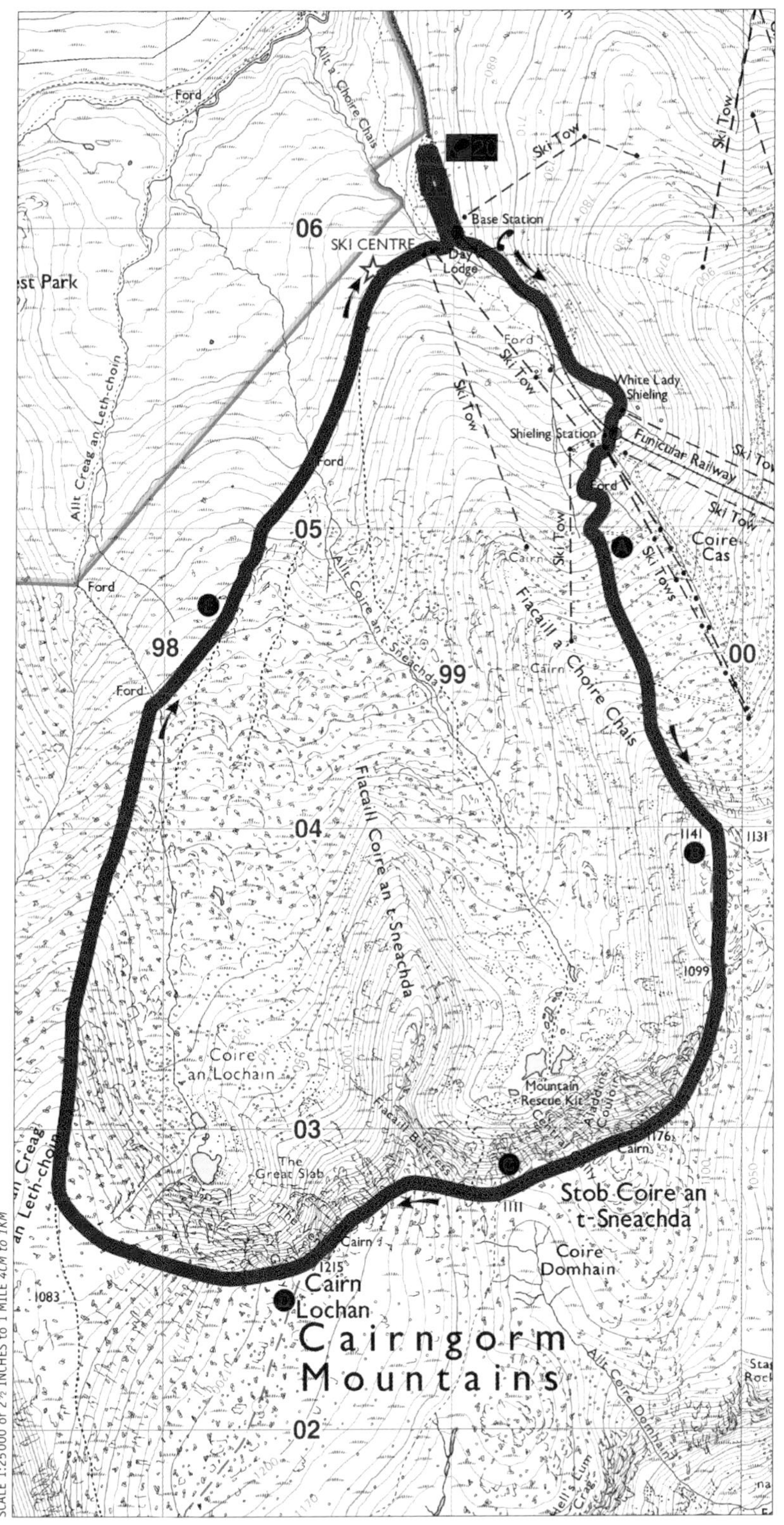

SCALE 1:25000 or 2½ INCHES to 1 MILE *4CM to 1KM*

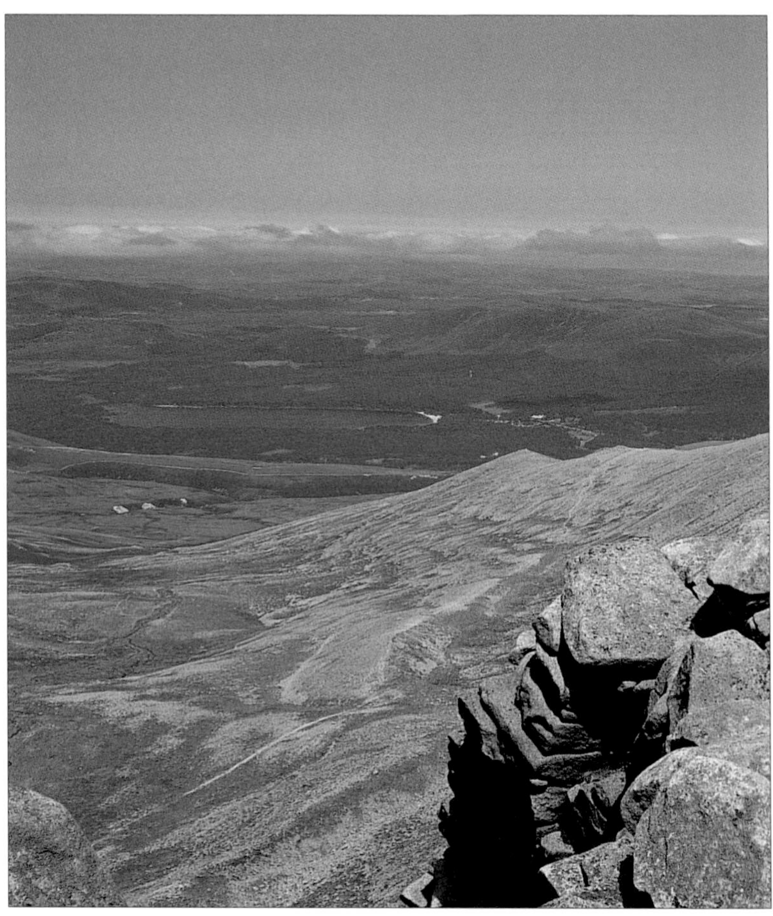

Loch Morlich and from Coire an t-Sneachda

path, however, take the lesser one ahead following cairns by the edge of Fiacaill Buttress and enjoying stupendous views northwards. On a good day you will be able to see the Sutherland mountains clearly and some have claimed to see the Cuillins of Skye from the Cairngorm summits. There is a cairn at the top of the buttress which is probably the best viewpoint on this route. Look to the left beyond the lochans on the floor of Coire an Lochain to see the homeward path.

A series of small cairns leads you around the rim of the corrie and up to the summit of Cairn Lochan **D** where the cairn itself (at 3986ft/1215m) is built very close to the edge of a sheer drop of 1000ft (304m) – a fact made all the more dramatic by the rock towers which overlook it. It is also worth looking southwards for a view of Ben Macdui, whose cairn should be quite clearly visible.

Leave the cairn and follow the rim of Coire an Lochain gradually turning towards the north west and still following cairns. Keep Coire an Lochain on your right and descend the easy ridge to the ford **E**. Continue to the second ford at the crossing of the Allt Coire an t-Sneachda. Many people come this far from the car park – it is just a few minutes walk from here to the starting point.

Morrone

Start	The Duck Pond, Braemar (take the Linn of Dee road but fork left at Airlie House and climb to the end of the road, Chapel Brae)
Distance	7 miles (11.25km)
Approximate time	3½ hours
Parking	At start
Refreshments	Pubs and cafés in Braemar
Ordnance Survey maps	Landranger 43 (Braemar & Blair Atholl), Explorer 404 (Braemar, Tomintoul, Glen Avon)

At 2815ft (859m) Morrone ('the big nose') is a fair way from being a Munro, yet it is still a considerable hill if only in terms of its bulk. It lies to the south of Braemar, a whaleback crowned with a radio mast which makes it unmistakable both from the village and more remote points such as the Linn of Quoich. In fact, on this route you only have to climb a little over 1600ft (490m) to the summit which is an excellent viewpoint for much of Deeside, Lochnagar and other major peaks of the Cairngorms. Note that if you take dogs on this walk you may have to lift them over the high stile at D.

The walk starts from the large car park by the duck pond at the end of Chapel Brae on the west side of Braemar. This is part of the village of Auchendryne which was originally separate from Castleton on the east side of the River Dee. The two places joined to establish Braemar ('the Brae of Mar') when royalty made the district popular. Walk past the pond on the track and bear left when this divides following a blue waymark.

The going becomes quite steep as the track passes a cottage (Woodhill). Bear left again after this and climb to a seat and a mountain indicator. The view takes in many of the peaks surrounding Braemar, the most notable being Ben Macdui and Braeriach to the north west. Some of the mountains shown on the indicator are not actually visible since it was designed to stand in a position about 55ft (17m) higher. This is a part of the Morrone Birkwood Nature Reserve and there is a noticeboard describing the wildlife that may be seen on the hill. It is claimed that this is the finest example of upland birchwood to be found in Britain. Geologically, Morrone is mainly of quartzite though there is also an outcrop of limestone.

Continue for 100 yds (91m) beyond the indicator and then take the path to the right A clearly marked first by a post and then by a cairn. The path climbs steadily and it is as well to pause occasionally to catch breath and take in the views to Braemar. The

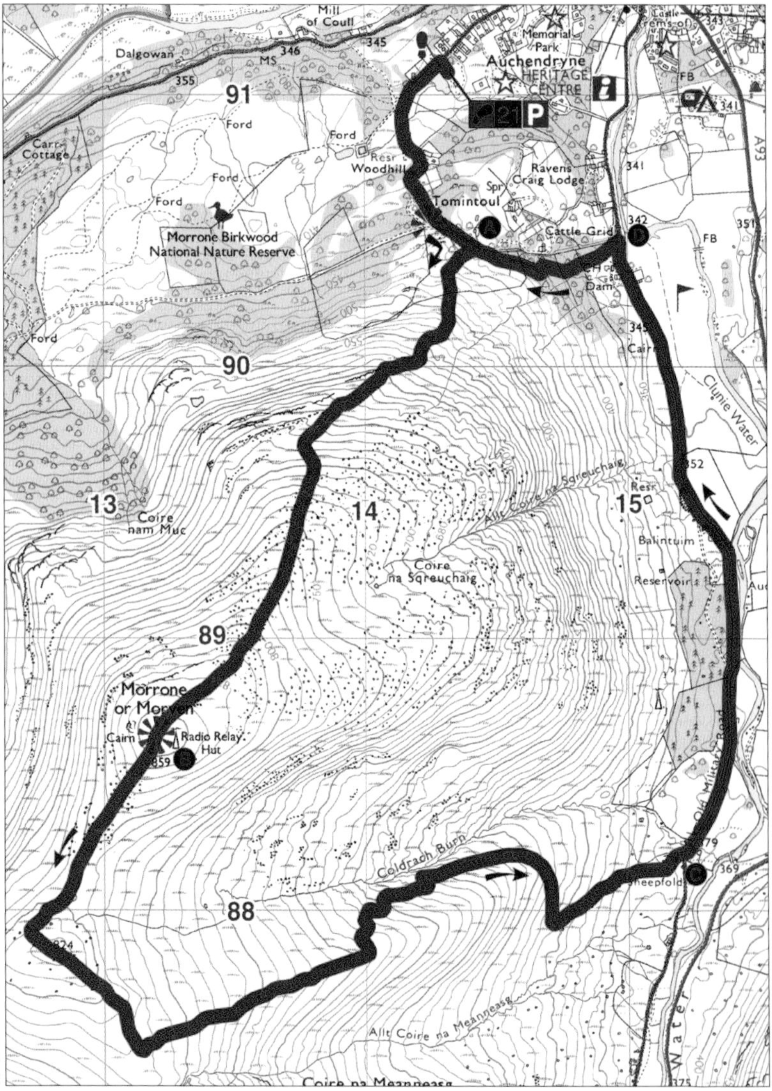

SCALE 1:27777 or about 2¾ INCHES to 1 MILE 3.6CM to 1KM

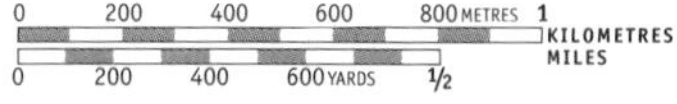

village is situated at a height of over 1000ft (305m) and is amongst the highest in Scotland. This altitude, combined with the surrounding hills which trap cold air, have bestowed on Braemar the unenviable record of having experienced the lowest temperature ever recorded in Britain, the -28°C (-18°F) which was reached in January 1982.

The vistas are even better after climbing beyond a deer fence with the famous Games Park clearly visible – this is where the Highland Gathering is held on the first weekend in September each year. The path strikes southwards up the broad shoulder of the hill and Braemar Castle appears neatly framed in a cleft of tree-clad hills. You may think that you are almost at the top when you reach a line of four cairns which might have once served as shooting butts. However, the summit is still about another $^1/_2$ mile (800m) ahead, though the worst of the climbing is now at an end.

The summit itself ● is bare, the only feature being the radio mast and the paraphernalia around it. Part of this is a weather recording centre, the readings from which are relayed to a noticeboard in Braemar village centre by the post office. By now Braemar is out of sight and the interest lies in attempting to identify the surrounding peaks.

Ben Avon with its distinctive tors is obvious to the north with Beinn a' Bhuird to the left, a more anonymous, broad-topped hill. Turning to the right there is a grand view down the River Dee with the magnificent face of Lochnagar overlooking it farther to the east. Loch Callater is obvious to the south east and its glen is followed by the famous Jock's Road via Fafernie and Tolmount, and then on into Glen Clova. To the south the shape of Cairnwell is unmistakable, while the climax of the scene comes with the major peaks of the Cairngorms arrayed to the north west.

Walk past the radio mast to the Land Rover track on the other side. This can be seen winding southwards over the hill. You will probably see more grouse on this hill (where they are protected) than on any of its neighbours.

Although the way is long it is never dreary with different views opening up all the time. When you reach the road ● turn left and walk by the Clunie Water to pass through the golf course. At the end of this, just before a cattle-grid, turn left ● and climb up steeply by a small caravan site to a deer fence (a dog would need to be exceptionally agile to climb the steps here). After crossing this take the path which still climbs, winding through a birch wood to a second fence. Here the path leaves the birches and there is an abandoned house to the right (Tomintoul). The path joins a track which leads past the path going up to Morrone ● and the mountain indicator encountered earlier. From here retrace your steps past Woodhill to return to the duck pond. ●

Braemar from Morrone

Cambus o' May and the Muir of Dinnet

Start	Dinnet, 6 miles (9.5km) west of Aboyne where the A97 crosses the A93
Distance	9 miles (14.5km)
Approximate time	4½ hours
Parking	Car park at Dinnet crossroads
Refreshments	Pub in Dinnet, tearoom at ●, hotel at Cambus o' May
Ordnance Survey maps	Landrangers 37 (Strathdon & Alford) and 44 (Ballater & Glen Clova), Explorer 388 (Lochnagar, Glen Muick & Glen Clova)

There are at least three contrasting landscapes to be enjoyed on this lengthy walk. First you pass through the flat landscape surrounding lochs Kinord and Davan, part of a nature reserve where birdwatchers will be in their element. These lochs are shallow and owe their origin to glacial deposits unlike the far deeper ones which nestle below Cairngorm peaks and were formed by glacial erosion. Later the route climbs the flank of Culblean Hill with its Scots' pines and silver birches before descending through forest to the disused railway line along wooded banks of the River Dee. Try to find time to visit the Burn o' Vat while you are here. The short walk will only take 30 minutes or so.

■ From the car park in the centre of Dinnet walk northwards on the A97 for about ½ mile (800m) before turning left ● on to a track into the Muir of Dinnet National Nature Reserve. *Note that the Nature Reserve bylaws require dogs to be on leads at all times in order to protect ground-nesting birds.*

The track crosses heathland before coming to the old schoolhouse which formerly served Dinnet even though it was about one mile (1.6km) from the village. School children used a more direct path but even so they often had to battle to their lessons through snow or driving rain. Turn right at the junction by the school ● on to the track which leads to the Warden's House at New Kinord.

Turn left at another T-junction ● to pass the house and continue through meadows which give pastoral views of Loch Kinord to the left. A Bronze Age crannog (a settlement on an artificial island) lies just offshore. Bear left and go through a metal gate where this track divides. It turns northwards away from the shore and the ruins of Old Kinord can be seen to the right. Bear left when the track from the old croft joins the path and cross beneath electricity cables, the first of several occasions on this walk when they provide a useful landmark. Loch Davan will now be seen to the right before trees hide it as the track wanders through birches and eventually reaches the main road. These shallow lochs are a haven for birdlife and are typical of those to be found in areas where, at the end of the last Ice Age, glaciers deposited their load of debris. Scottish Natural Heritage hope to provide a birdwatching hide at one of the lochs shortly.

Cambus o' May bridge

Bear right and follow the path for about 400 yds (366m) to a road junction **B** where the road to Raebush goes ahead and leaves the B9119. Turn left here to take a track which divides after 50 yds (46m). Take the lesser track here to the left which passes through woods at first before climbing on to the heather-covered hill. This is Culblean Hill where the Battle of Culblean was fought in 1335 – a significant victory for the Scots under Sir Andrew de Moray over the English troops of the Earl of Atholl (who died on the battlefield). Culblean marked the turning point in the Second Scottish War of Independence which kept the 11-year-old King David II on the Scottish throne – though the King himself actually lived safely in France throughout the campaign.

The track climbs steadily and it is as well to pause occasionally to catch breath and take in the glorious views northwards. You pass beneath the power lines again. Young pine trees growing in the middle of the track show how quickly the way could become lost. Eventually the climbing ends and the valley of the Vat Burn is to the left as more power lines come into view. The track descends to ford the little Vat Burn, then comes to a deer gate and a Muir of Dinnet National Nature Reserve noticeboard. You leave the reserve at this point to enter Forest Enterprise land.

The track soon heads southwards through the forest. Bear left when it divides following a yellow waymark. At a cattle-grid the forest walks are waymarked off to the right but this route crosses the grid and remains on the track. It reaches the main road close to The Cranach coffee shop. Cross the road to the trackbed of the old railway **C** which now serves as a footpath and cycle track. Turn left and enjoy the level walking on a good surface. The river is close to the right as you pass Turner Hall Hotel and a mile or so further on you will reach the Cambus o' May Hotel where the path turns off the track momentarily before rejoining it to pass the beautiful suspension bridge

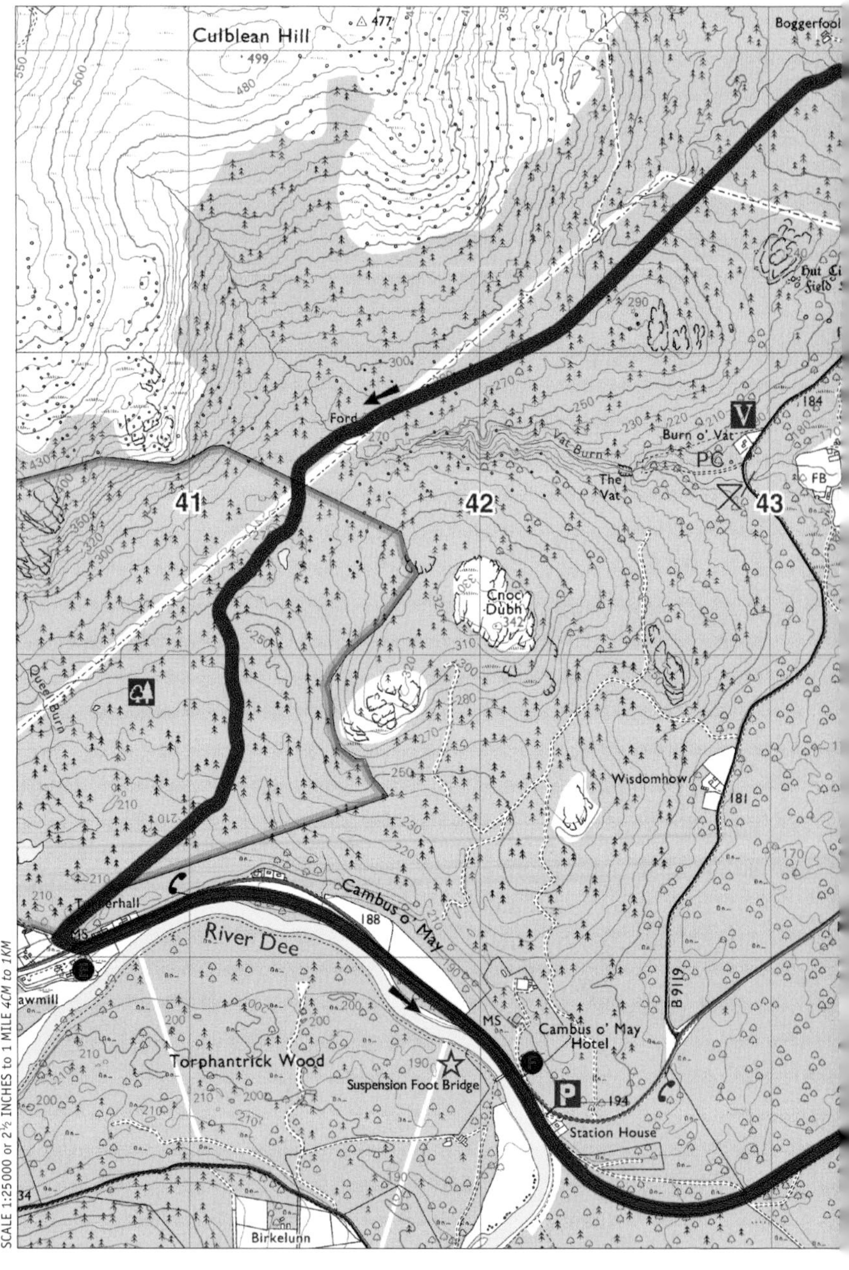

0 200 400 600 800 METRES 1 KILOMETRES
0 200 400 600 YARDS ½ MILES

● and then the former station, now restored to serve as a private dwelling.

After the station the old railway leaves the river and, after a bridge, runs in an almost straight line for nearly two miles (3.2km). There is a steady climb at first and one can easily imagine the fireman's anxiety in the days of steam as he tried to keep a good fire burning from Cambus o' May. The hills are vaguely seen through the birches to the right

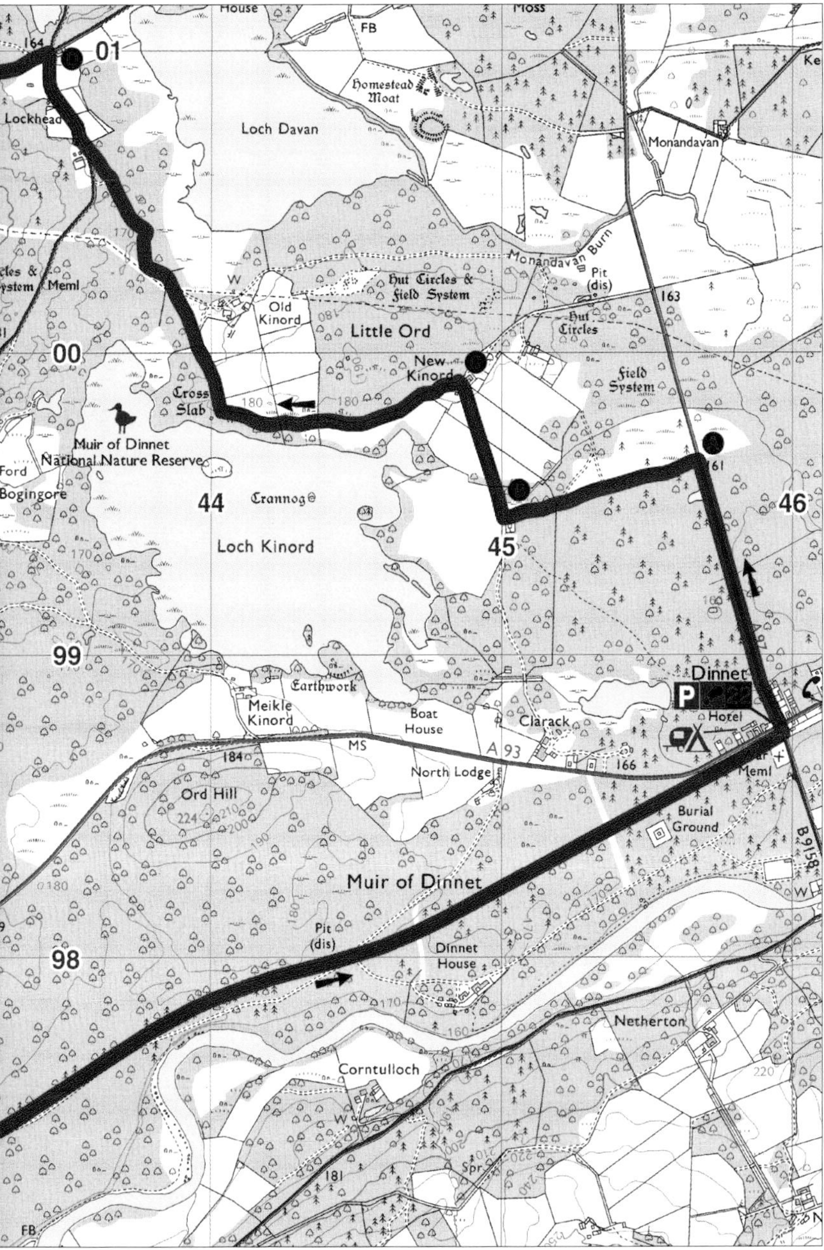

and there is also a fine view back towards the Cairngorms. As you near Dinnet the way passes through the heart of the Muir of Dinnet, a wide glacial basin overlooked by fine hills where the birch scrub and heather are particularly attractive in late summer and autumn. Dinnet itself was a village which sprang from the coming of the railway. Its only other claim to fame was that, at the age of eight, Lord Byron spent time at a nearby farm recovering from scarlet fever. The former railway brings you back to the centre of the village opposite the starting point. ●

Gleann Einich

Start	Whitewell, at the end of the road from Inverdruie
Distance	12½ miles (20km)
Approximate time	6½ hours
Parking	On the common before Whitewell Do not obstruct the turning area
Refreshments	None
Ordnance Survey maps	Landranger 36 (Grantown & Aviemore), Explorer 403 (Cairngorm & Aviemore)

This is a long walk into the heart of the western Cairngorms through the Rothiemurchus pine forest and one of the finest glens to Loch Einich. Navigation is straightforward as the route lies on paths and tracks. However, the higher section beyond the forest has no shelter in bad weather and, after heavy rain or rapid thaw, some of the burn crossings may be difficult. Also snow can lie very deep here well into spring, hiding the path. In such conditions it would be inadvisable to venture beyond point D.

Walk eastwards from the road at Whitewell and descend to the track coming from Coylumbridge. Turn right on to this and follow it for ½ mile (800m) to a crossways A. Keep ahead here, following the sign to Loch Einich and with the attractive Lochan Deò to the left. After roughly 100 yds (91m) pass through a gate which is also marked to Loch Einich at a point where a track comes in from the right. To the left the scattered mature Scots' pines have abundant young trees below them. These are self sown trees and are the natural continuation of the 8000-year-old forest. About ¾ mile (1.2km) farther on the first of half a dozen or so burns crosses the path.

At B cross another burn and continue ahead following the sign 'Footpath and Cyclists'. A steep track goes off to the right here. On the left a striking row of dead pines overlooks the burn. For a while beyond this point the path runs almost level along the east-facing side of a steep slope. The pines to the left are exceptionally fine with both wet and dry areas beneath them, hummocky ground supporting bracken and blaeberries. The occasional large dead pine is a vital part of the forest habitat; crested tits, special birds of the pine forest, will only nest in such trees. Their spluttering trill can often be heard along this section of the route. Am Beanaidh, the river flowing from Loch Einich, can be heard rushing down the glen. Directly ahead the cone of Carn Eilrig fills the view with pines reaching high up its slopes.

Where Am Beanaidh comes into view there is a fine stand of alders and rowan growing around an island

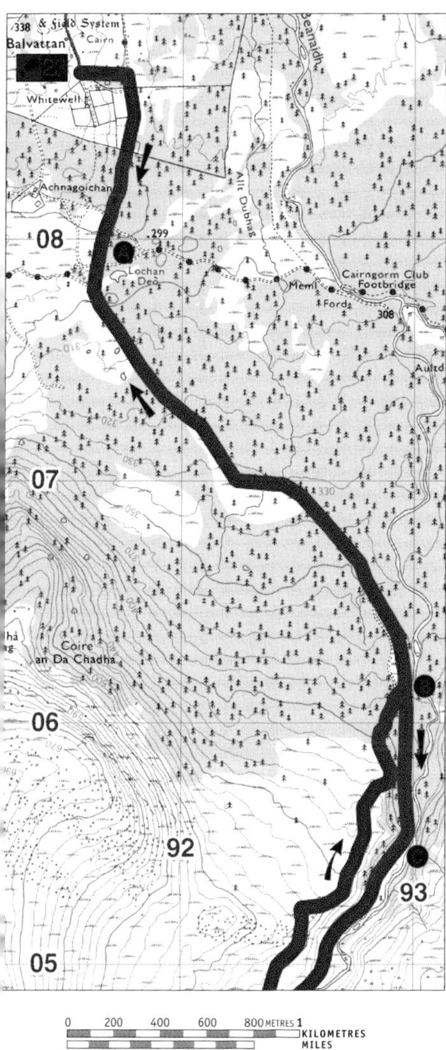

in the river. Beyond, the pinewood rises to blend into a solid mass of deep blue-green. In one place the path crosses a steep loose slope of exposed sands and gravels left by the ice sheet as it melted thousands of years ago.

The path turns a sharp corner at ●. Ahead the forest is suddenly reduced to the narrow confines of the burn while beyond is the first glimpse of open country. Continue to ● where the track which left the route at ● rejoins. Here are the last few pines of the forest. Tradition has it that, in the spring, cattle used to be driven to this point and would then make their own way up Gleann Einich for the summer, to be followed later by the herdsmen and their families who lived in shielings (rough huts) in the glen throughout the summer. In the far

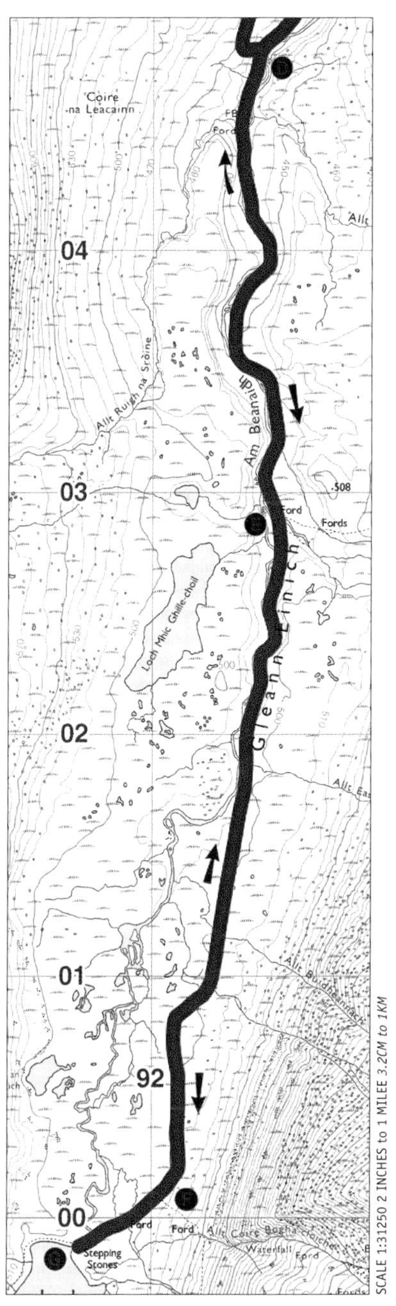

distance steep ridges and cliffs below Sgoran Dubh Mór can be seen.

Continue southwards along the track and in about 500 yds (457m) cross a footbridge over Am Beanaidh.

At E you have to ford the Beanaidh Bheag which is a sizeable burn draining the high corries of Braeriach. It may well be necessary to detour upstream to find a crossing place. In spate it may not be possible to cross and you will be forced to turn back. Ahead Gleann Einich is dramatic with the mountains closing in. The route south finally leaves the confines of the glacial terraces and runs in a straight line over gently undulating ground. In autumn red deer congregate here, the hoarse bellowing of the stags echoing from the hills. By staying on the track you will be able to watch them without causing any disturbance.

Loch Einich finally comes into view as a sliver of silver at the head of the glen. On the right the cliffs and gullies below Sgoran Dubh and Sgor Gaoith can be seen. In the early part of this century these cliffs were popular with Cairngorm mountaineers but in recent decades they have fallen out of favour, other steeper cliffs at higher altitudes providing greater challenges. The track detours left to avoid an extensive area of peat bog. Hundreds of pine stumps and roots can be seen here. These are several thousand years old and show the height at which the trees thrived formerly before the climate became cooler and wetter, and peat prevented the growth of young trees.

At F a tumbledown cairn marks the point at which an old stalkers' path branches off to the left. If you climb a little way up this path you will see a fine series of waterfalls, though beyond this the path climbs high into the hills and is only a route for the experienced and well-equipped walker.

Continuing on the main track you finally reach Loch Einich G. About 1½ miles (2.4km) long, the loch provides the main drinking supply for Strathspey. The water here is clear because of the very low level of nutrients,which is the result of rainwater draining off the surrounding hills of bare granite. The cliffs at the head of the loch are an important site for some of the less common Cairngorm flowers and scrub willows.

Gleann Einich

The return to Whitewell is by the same route, though at D you should follow the track up to the left if you want to get the best views back up the glen. This path rejoins the outward route at B. The descent into the shelter of the pine forest makes a fine end to a long day. ●

Bynack More from Glenmore

Start	Allt Mor car park
Distance	14 miles (22.5km)
Approximate time	7 hours
Parking	Free parking at start
Refreshments	None
Ordnance Survey maps	Landranger 36 (Grantown & Aviemore), Explorer 403 (Cairngorm & Aviemore)

The approach and walk out is on well defined forest roads. However, the ascent and descent of Bynack More is a demanding hill walk on a rough path and open moor. The final half mile (800m) to the summit traverses a fine ridge which is interesting but without any difficulties in summer. The summit reveals splendid views over Loch Avon and the central Cairngorm Mountains. This is a strenuous walk, which should only be attempted in good weather.

■ From the Allt Mor car park head off in a south-easterly direction indicated by a yellow marker post. Almost immediately cross the narrow timber footbridge over the Allt Mor. (The footbridge can be seen from the car park.) After crossing the bridge turn left, the path soon becomes a forest road.

After about 500 yds (458m) another forest road goes left, keep straight on here, all tracks are indicated with yellow marker posts. A metal 'Bailey' bridge over the Alt na Ciste is crossed.

At ● the track divides to form a turning loop for forestry vehicles. Turn right, pass the yellow marker post, and soon turn right again onto a path by another yellow marker. This path passes over a footbridge in order to avoid the ford across the Allt Ban. After the bridge the path joins a forest road, turn left, then immediately right to rejoin the main track. Another yellow marker post confirms the way.

At ● turn right. You now follow blue markers to Lochan Uaine, the Green Lochan. This beautiful lochan takes its colour from the surrounding Scots Pine woodland. Rest awhile here on your return. Follow the main track past the lochan and turn right at the fork in about 400 yds (366m). Note the views over Loch a Gharbh-choire towards Abernethy Forest.

The track becomes rough and wet on the approach to ● Bynack Stable. This cannot be relied upon for shelter as its removal is under review, if it doesn't blow down first! Cross the bridge over the River Nethy and commence the steady climb up the obvious but rough path ahead. This path leads eventually to the Lairig an Laoigh, a route right through the Caingorm mountains to rival the better known Lairig Ghru.

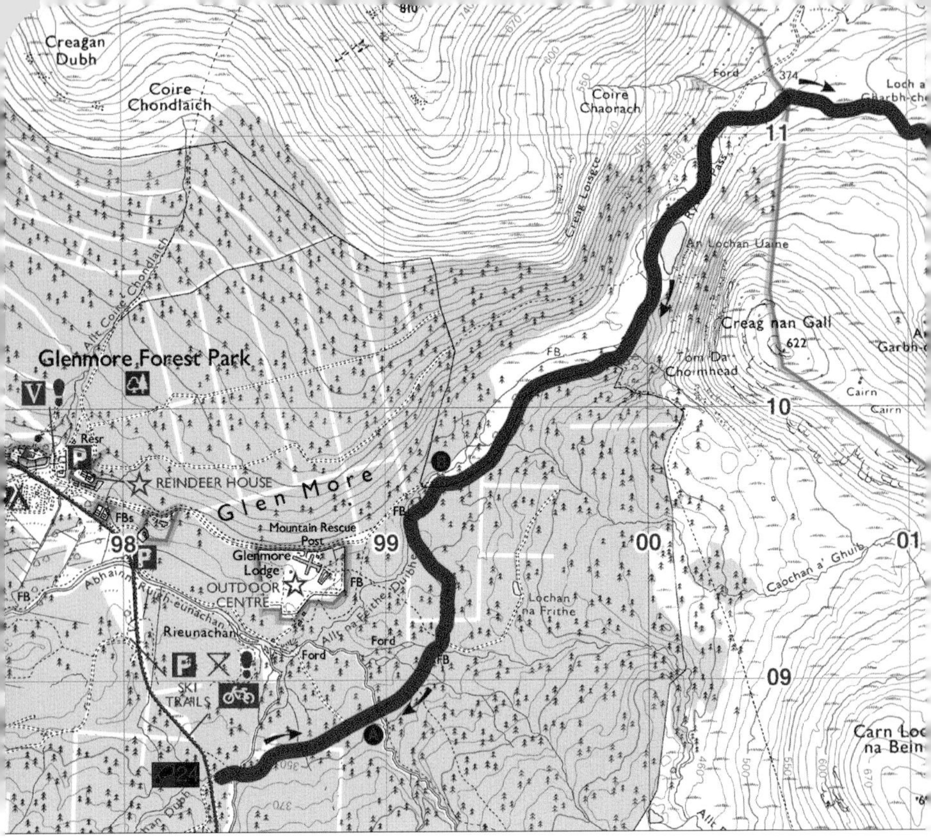

The path levels out and divides. Both become vague. The Lairig an Laoigh path swings away to the east and starts to descend. Our path crosses spot height 818m (2683ft) from which the main ridge of Bynack More rises dead ahead. The first few feet of the ridge is up steep grass after which the gradient eases. The ridge is boulder strewn on the right and rocky on the left. The crest is not sharp and provides an interesting and relatively safe route to the top. At last the summit is reached and only in the last few yards is the

Bynack More

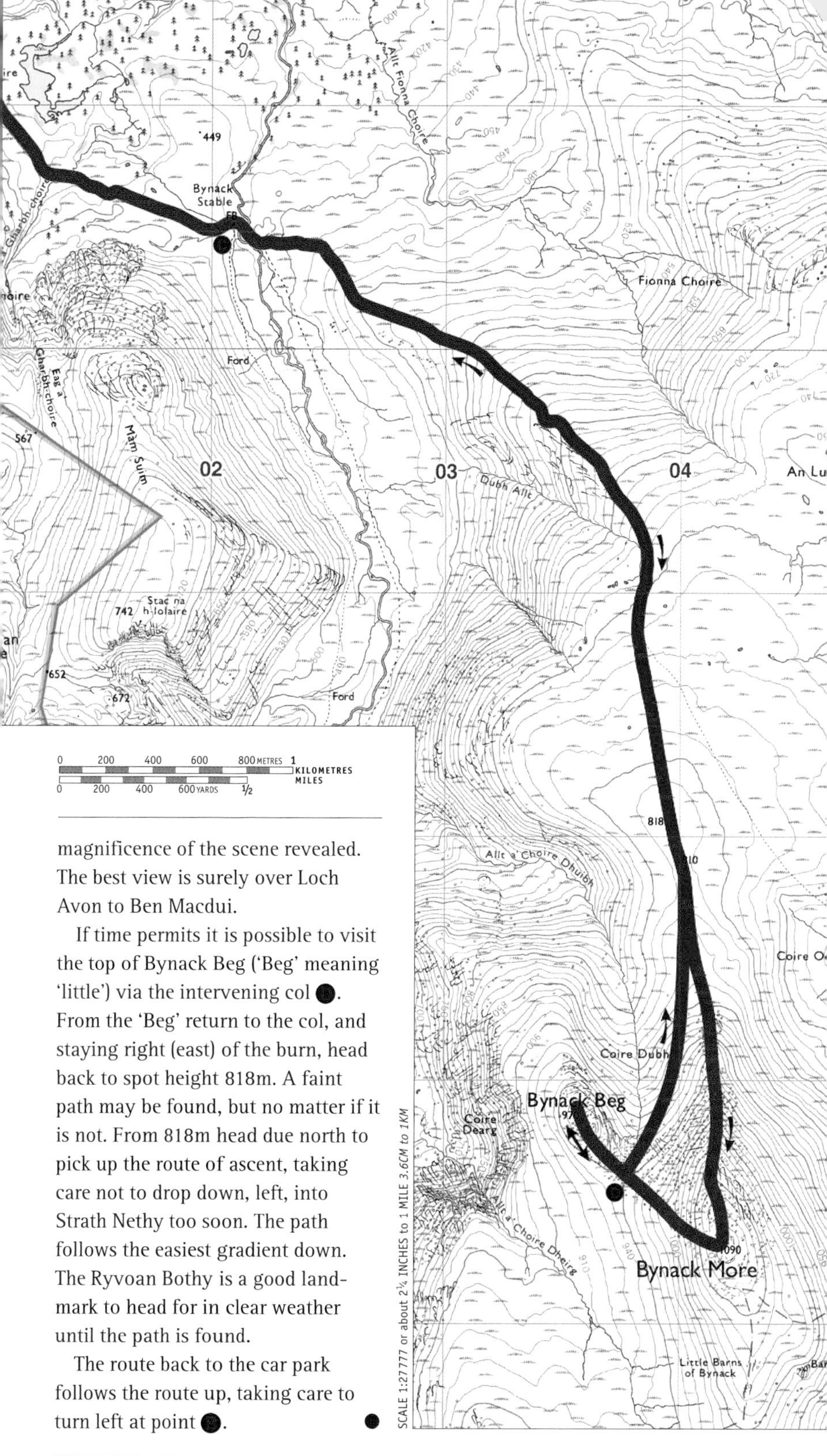

magnificence of the scene revealed. The best view is surely over Loch Avon to Ben Macdui.

If time permits it is possible to visit the top of Bynack Beg ('Beg' meaning 'little') via the intervening col ●. From the 'Beg' return to the col, and staying right (east) of the burn, head back to spot height 818m. A faint path may be found, but no matter if it is not. From 818m head due north to pick up the route of ascent, taking care not to drop down, left, into Strath Nethy too soon. The path follows the easiest gradient down. The Ryvoan Bothy is a good landmark to head for in clear weather until the path is found.

The route back to the car park follows the route up, taking care to turn left at point ●. ●

Carn an Fhreiceadain from Kingussie

Start	From near the top of West Terrace, Kingussie (the road to the golf course). Look for a path to the right leading to a footbridge
Distance	9½ miles (15.25km)
Approximate time	4 hours
Parking	Roadside parking at start
Refreshments	Pubs and cafés in Kingussie
Ordnance Survey maps	Landranger 52 (Pitlochry & Crieff), Explorer 402 (Badenoch & Upper Strathspey)

Most of this walk is on well-defined tracks, though there is rough walking across heather for about one mile (1.6km) as you begin the descent from Carn an Fhreiceadain. The walk is a good introduction to the Monadhliath Mountains which lie to the west of the A9, an area neglected by many in favour of the popular Cairngorm routes. Although these summits lack the splendour of those to the east they provide fine viewpoints and you are unlikely to encounter anyone else in the course of the walk in this desolate but beautiful wilderness. In the shooting season ring 01540 661237 to make certain of safe access.

A Cross the footbridge and turn left on to the road which is private after gates as it approaches the golf course with the Gynack Burn close to the left. Keep an eye open for ill-struck golfballs as you pass by some of the outlying tees and greens. The surfaced track continues to climb beyond the top of the golf course but ends at a bridge **B** by a large cream coloured building with a curved roof. Do not cross the bridge but turn right up the track which follows the burn.

The plantations end and the track passes through a gate. Another gate takes the track on to the open hill. Already there is a fine view back with Creag Bheag well seen to the south as you climb higher. This is the peak to the south of Loch Gynack, not the lesser hill with the same name immediately to the east of the track. Creag Mhór is the rugged summit to the right as you look back with Creag Dhubh the higher peak a little way to the north. 'Creag Dhubh' is the battle-cry of the Clan Macpherson but it refers to the hill of the same name which rises to the south west and overlooks Cluny Castle, once the headquarters of the clan. There is an abundance of foxgloves and juniper bushes by the track whose purpose is

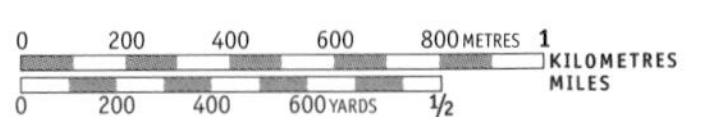

SCALE 1:27777 or about 2¼ INCHES to 1 MILE 3.6CM to 1KM

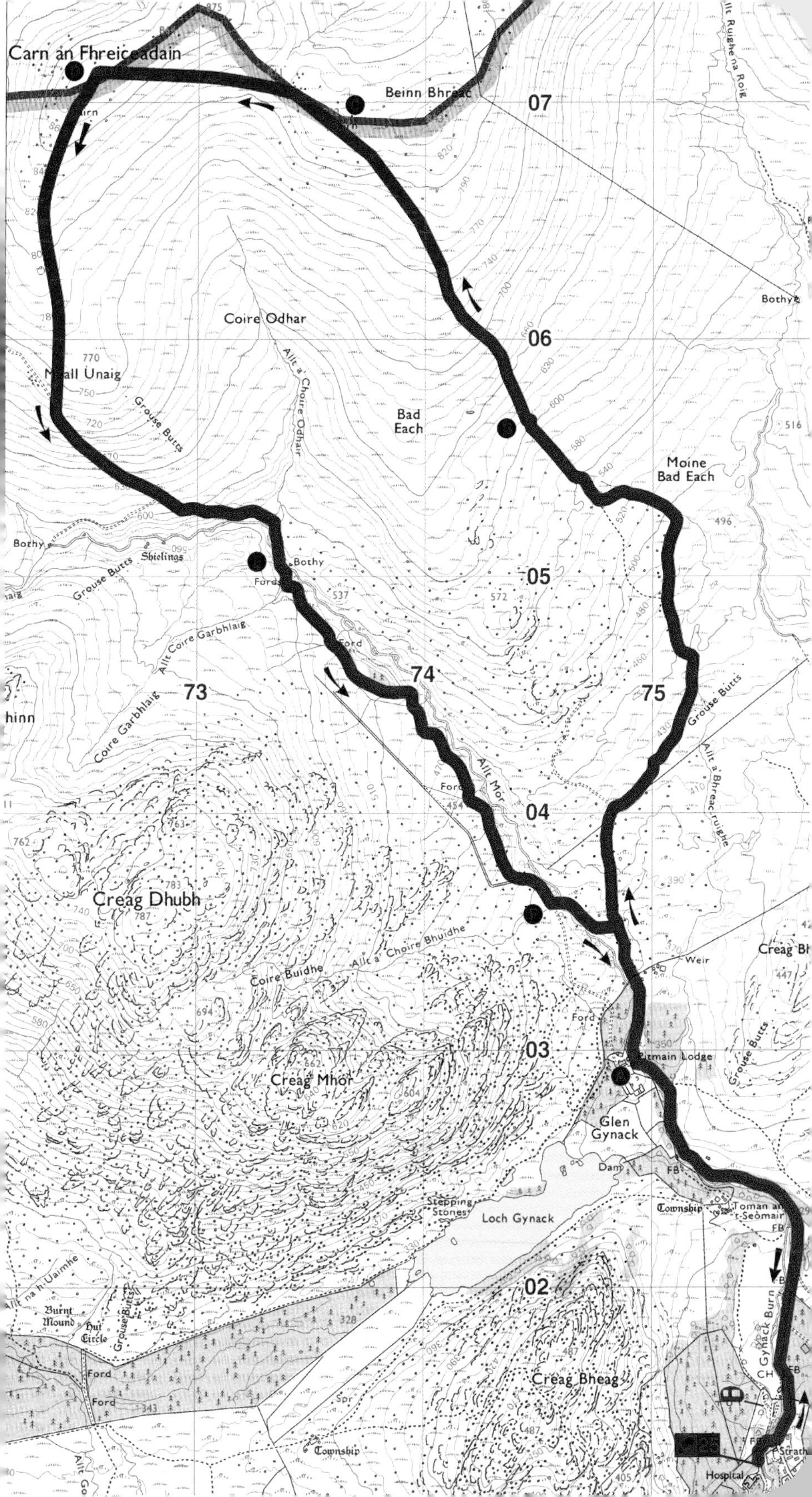

Carn an Fhreiceadain
Beinn Bhreac
07
Allt Ruighe na Roig
Coire Odhar
Allt a' Choire Odhair
06
Bad Each
Meall Unaig
Grouse Butts
Moine Bad Each
Bothy
Shielings
Ford
05
Allt Coire Garbhlaig
Coire Garbhlaig
73
74
75
Allt Mor
04
Allt a' Bhreac-ruighe
Creag Dhubh
Allt a' Choire Bhuidhe
Coire Buidhe
Weir
Creag Mhor
03
Pitmain Lodge
Glen Gynack
Dam
FB
Township
Toman an t-Seomair
Stepping Stones
Loch Gynack
Allt na h-Uamhe
02
Burnt Mound
Hut Circle
Creag Bheag
Gynack Burn
CH
Spr
Hospital
Strath

The track to Beinn Bhreac

made clear as the first of a series of grouse butts comes into view. The sheep on this hill are a distinctive breed which look as though they have goat genes in their ancestry.

The gradient becomes severe after the track runs past a wooden hut B but then eases off a little when the track comes to an end near the summit of Beinn Bhreac. Wheeled vehicles have a choice of routes here over the gritty surface.

It takes about two hours to reach the cairn on Beinn Bhreac at 2730ft (832m) C which is located just to the west of the summit. It is a wonderful viewpoint over miles of barren hills to the west while the majestic peaks of the Cairngorms are well seen to the north east. From here walk one mile (1.6km) or so westwards on a vague track to the neighbouring summit of Carn an Fhreiceadain (2880ft/878m) which has a triangulation pillar and a very distinctive cairn, both of which are usually visible on the skyline, the latter D being some distance farther on to the south west. The name of the hill reflects its excellence as a viewpoint – translated from the Gaelic it means 'the lookout cairn'.

The Monadhliaths ('grey mountains') form part of the southern Grampians but contrast with the Cairngorms which also belong to this group and face them across the valley of the Spey. Where the latter are steep-sided and craggy the Monadhliath peaks are comparatively low and uniform with rare outcrops of rock. Few paths other than stalkers' tracks penetrate Byron's 'irksome solitudes' and thus they remain unexplored by most walkers.

The track continues westwards from the summit but it is easy to save distance by following it for about ½ mile (800m) and then turning off to the left to follow a line of old posts to the top of a spur, Meall Unaig. From here descend the slopes to join the track by Allt Unaig which is more substantial after a bridge E where it becomes the Allt Mór.

The way back from here to Glen Gynack is very enjoyable. When the track descends to the treeline look for an easy way to cross the burn. One opportunity occurs as it straightens and runs close to the stream F which is easily fordable unless there has been a recent prolonged downpour. Once across the stream follow the outward route back to Kingussie. ●

Sron na Lairige and Braeriach from Loch an Eilein

Start	Loch an Eilein car park (nominal charge in summer)
Distance	18 miles (28.8km)
Approximate time	8 to 10 hours
Parking	At start
Refreshments	None
Ordnance Survey maps	Landranger 36 (Grantown & Aviemore), Explorers 387 (Glen Shee & Braemar) and 403 (Cairngorm & Aviemore)

This is a long and arduous walk, which should only be attempted in favourable summer conditions, and with an early start. It features the traditional Cairngorm 'long walk in' giving a feeling of commitment and remoteness to the walk. The approach is through beautiful open Scots Pine forest, which gives way to the heavily glaciated northern end of the Lairig Ghru. The real climbing starts some six miles (9.6km) into the walk, up the northern slopes of Sron na Lairige. The walk may be terminated on this first summit, reducing the distance by a couple of miles. An alternative start from Whitewell will save a further mile or so (see Walk 23 and map). A further option, from the summit of Braeriach is to continue over Einich Cairn. The descent into Gleann Einich is by the stalker's path at the head of the glen, returning as Walk 23, adding about four miles (6.4km) to the total.

Whichever option is chosen, be prepared to turn back at any point, do not over extend yourself, and keep an eye on the time! IMPORTANT NOTE! – Older maps may show the Sinclair Memorial Hut at the start of the Lairig Ghru. This has been demolished and there is no shelter here.

■ From Loch an Eilein car park head out the way you drove in, cross the bridge and turn immediately right, signposted 'Public Footpath to Braemar by the Lairig Ghru'. Continue above the north eastern shore of the loch.

A footbridge ● is reached 10 yds (9m) before a junction. Turn left here signposted 'Lairig Ghru and Gleann Einich'. The next two fords are bridged. Here we pass through some of the most beautiful Scots Pine

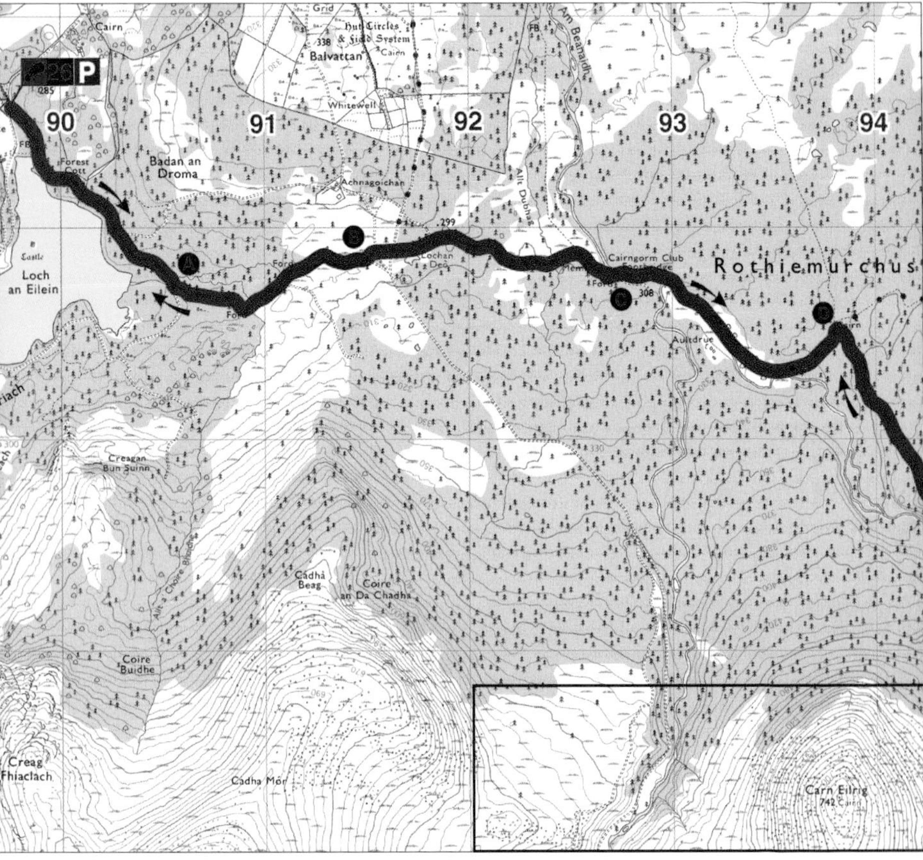

0 200 400 600 800 METRES 1 KILOMETRES
MILES
0 200 400 600 YARDS ½

SCALE 1:25 714 or about 1¾ INCHES to 1 MILE 2.8CM to 1KM

woodland in Scotland with views to Cairngorm and Cairn Lochan ahead.

At B a fork in the path is reached. Keep left as signposted 'Cyclists'. After 50 yds the path forks again, keep right. After 30 yds there is a crossroads of paths, go straight on (the main Gleann Einich track is visible from here). After a farther 75 yds the main Gleann Einich track is reached, go straight across into the trees, signposted Lairig Ghru. (The track from Whitewell comes in from the left here.) The path continues with Lochan Deo on the right.

Keep a look out for the Cairngorm Club Footbridge at C, this is 20 yds to the left of our path. Cross the bridge, noting the date the bridge was built, and also the distances and times to various places from this point, and turn right.

At point D turn right. The Lairig Ghru path is signposted and marked with a low cairn of boulders, neither of which are too obvious! The path is narrower and rough now as it climbs above the Allt Druidh, which is seen down to the right through the trees.

As the trees thin out a knoll, actually a ridge of glacial moraine, provides a good stopping place, with views back over the forest to Aviemore and far beyond. As progress is made towards the Lairig Ghru a path joins from the left from Rothiemurchus Lodge.

At E the site of the (now demolished) Sinclair Hut is reached. Another path joins from the left, this

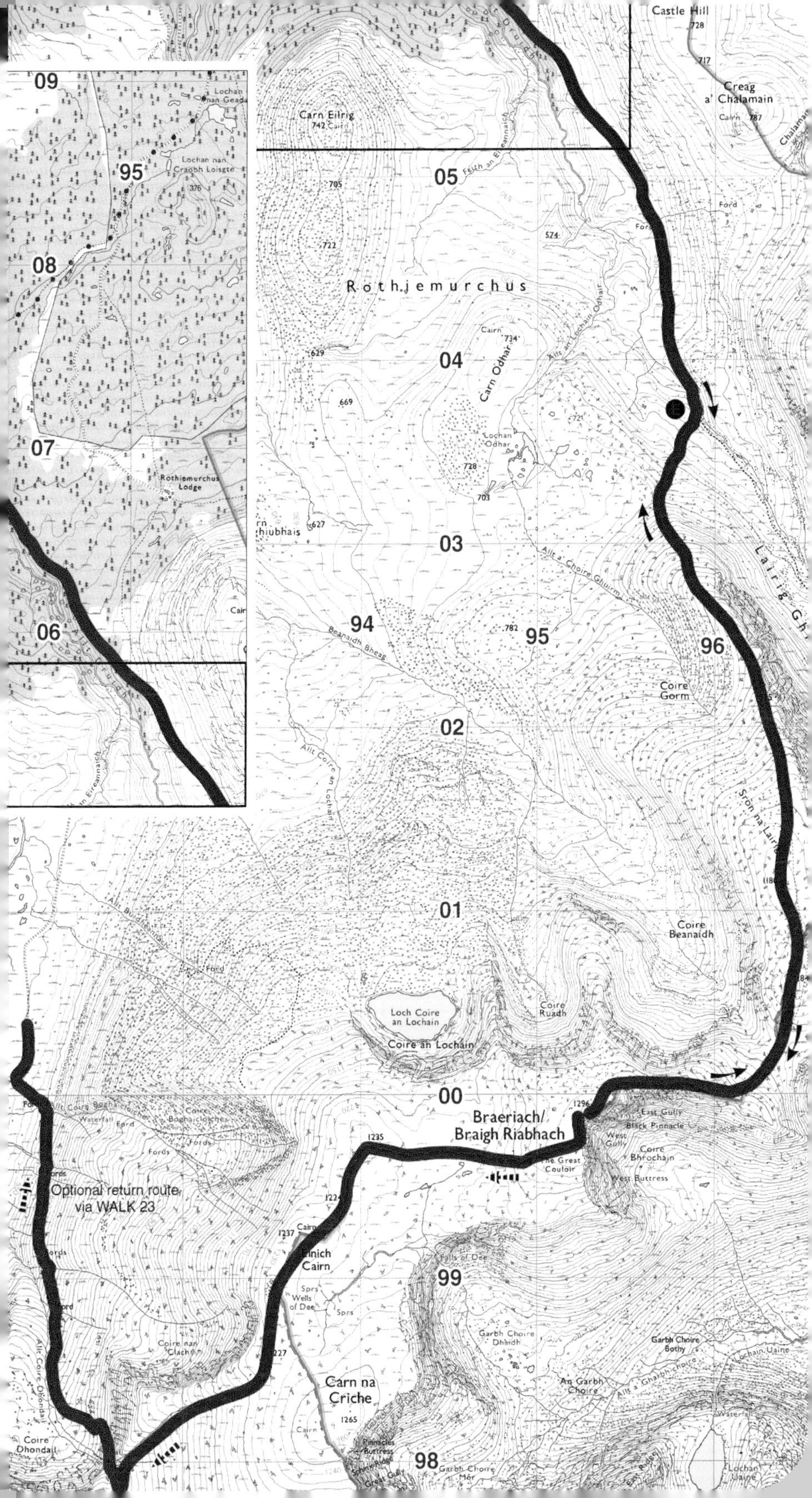

Castle Hill
Creag a' Chalamain
Carn Eilrig
Rothjemurchus
Lochan nan Geadas
Lochan nan Craobh Loisgte
Rothiemurchus Lodge
Carn Odhar
Lochan Odhar
Allt a' Choire Ghuirm
Lairig Ghru
Coire Gorm
Beanaidh Bheag
Allt Coire an Lochain
Sron na Lairige
Coire Beanaidh
Loch Coire an Lochain
Coire an Lochain
Coire Ruadh
Braeriach/
Braigh Riabhach
East Gully
Black Pinnacle
West Gully
Coire Bhrochain
The Great Couloir
West Buttress
Coire Bogha-cloiche
Optional return route via WALK 23
Einich Cairn
Wells of Dee
Falls of Dee
Garbh Choire Dhaidh
Garbh Choire Bothy
An Garbh Choire
Allt a' Gharbh-choire
Coire nan Clach
Carn na Criche
Allt Coire Dhondail
Coire Dhondail
Garbh Choire Mòr
Lochan Uaine
Ford
Fords
Waterfall
Cairn
09
08
07
06
05
04
03
02
01
00
99
98
94
95
96

time from the Chalamain Gap, a glacial overflow. Lurcher's Crag looms high on our left. Turn right, cross the burn and head for the base of Sron na Lairige. After about 300 yds (270m) turn left and head up the lower slopes of Sron na Lairige, keeping the steep drop over crags into the Lairig Ghru always on the left. Head for spot height 1180m (3870ft), the ridge broadens into a plateau, then over the summit at spot height 1184m. Drop down a little to the col between Coire Beabaidh and Coire Ruadh, then ascend the final easy slopes to the summit of Braeriach.

An Garbh Choire lies to the left. It is one of the finest corries in Scotland, being some 1500 ft (475m) deep to the main river, and about half that depth to the floor of the several upper corries, from the surrounding rim of cliffs.

The most impressive feature visible from the summit is the sheer area of land between 3000 and 4000 feet above sea level. Here one can fully appreciate the extent of the Cairngorm plateau and how the Lairig Ghru so dramatically divides it. The return route follows the route of ascent all the way back to the car park, with spectacular views over Strathspey being ahead for almost the whole way.

(If time and fitness permit, it is possible to extend this walk by continuing over Einich Cairn to the south west of Braeriach, carefully locating the stalker's path descending into Coire Dhondail, and returning by Walk 23. Caution should be exercised in selecting this option in wet weather or snowmelt, as there are a couple of sizeable fords in Gleann Einich.) ●

Lurcher's Crag from Sron na Lairige

The Lairig Ghru

Start	Whitewell, at the end of the road from Inverdruie
Distance	12½ miles (20km)
Approximate time	7 hours
Parking	Whitewell (but avoid parking in the turning space)
Refreshments	None
Ordnance Survey maps	Landranger 36 (Grantown & Aviemore), Explorers 387 (Glen Shee & Braemar) and 403 (Cairngorm & Aviemore)

This long walk should only be attempted in good conditions when the higher parts are certain to be clear of snow (which may last into May or even June). *It climbs through the ancient Rothiemurchus pine forest to the rocky pass of Lairig Ghru (which ultimately leads to Braemar). This route turns off the Lairig Ghru shortly before the summit to visit two more spectacular passes – the Chalamain Gap and Eag a' Chait – before returning via Rothiemurchus Lodge. Bad visibility would not only make navigation difficult (though there are few places where the path might be missed) but would also deny you views of some of the best Cairngorm scenery.*

The road to Whitewell provides popular wayside picnic places and is also a convenient starting point for expeditions into the hills.

A From the end of the road, turn left to head downhill on a rough path. Turn right when you meet a major path and go through an ordinary gate and then a kissing-gate in a deer fence to leave the Rothiemurchus Estate. A path leaves to the left soon after this but continue to a crossroads **B** and turn left there.

This path passes the tree-fringed Lochan Deò and wanders through a picturesque part of the ancient Rothiemurchus pine forest before it meets with the Lairig Ghru coming from Coylum Bridge. Bear right here towards the sound of rushing water and the Cairngorm Club Footbridge, which spans the Am Beanaidh and dates from 1912. Once over the bridge, follow the river upstream past an idyllic shady spot where the Allt Druidh joins it. The path follows this tributary closely at first but then swings left and climbs to a forest crossroads known as Piccadilly **C**.

The Lairig Ghru near the end of the pine forest

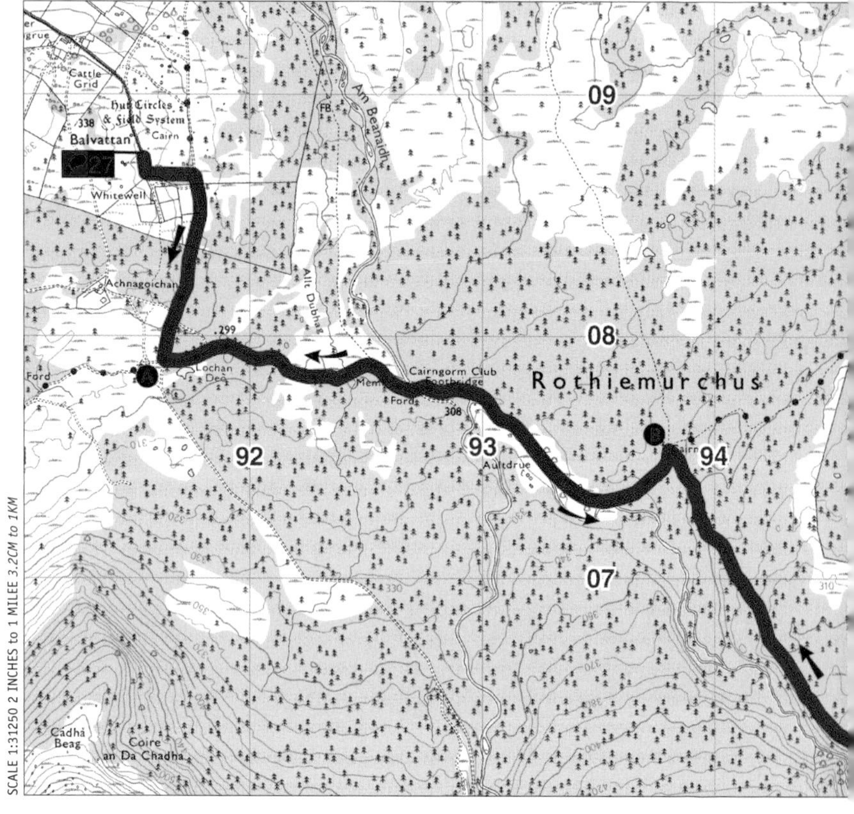

0 200 400 600 800 METRES 1 KILOMETRES
0 200 400 600 YARDS ½ MILES

Turn right here to pass the cairn following the sign to Lairig Ghru on a path which climbs gradually through the trees above Allt Druidh. As you climb the Scots' pines become smaller and more sparse. Look back for fine views with the buildings of Aviemore just discernible in the distance.

After about an hour you reach the point C where a path from Rothiemurchus Lodge joins from the left. From here the going becomes tougher with loose rocks underfoot and a steeper gradient. The path can be seen for a mile or so ahead climbing steadily towards a cleft in the hills. There is a brief view to the right of the Braeriach corries before they are hidden by the steep slopes which crowd in on the Lairig Ghru. The path runs by the burn once more and crosses D another coming up from the Chalamain Gap and continuing on the other side to the summit of Braeriach.

There is an option at D. The route is actually to the left here, up the path which climbs between Lurcher's Crag (to the right) and Creag a' Chalamain (to the left). *However, if time and energy allow you may like to go another $2\frac{1}{2}$ miles (4km) up the Lairig Ghru to the crest of the pass and look southwards into Glen Dee.*

From D the route continues steeply up a path which has recently been repaired to climb like a staircase for a little way. Look back for a view of the Lairig Ghru under the massive whale-back of Ben Macdui. The path crosses a boggy stretch before climbing again to the boulder-filled Chalamain Gap. Once at the summit of this pass, the path winds ahead towards the mountain road. It descends through more peat bogs; the tree roots are relics of the ancient pine forest. The path ends its gentle descent to climb steeply after crossing a burn. Turn left ● immediately after this stream on to a path which follows the watercourse. Look left for a view of the Chalamain Gap. Again, as you reach the summit of this pass, Eag a' Chait, progress is slowed by boulders. At the summit there is a tremendous view over Loch Morlich to Aviemore. The next objective, Rothiemurchus Lodge, can be seen with Loch an Eilein beyond.

The path descends steeply with a fence to the right. The ground is very boggy just before the Lodge and the path ends near the helicopter pad. Follow the roadway to a bell which commemorates the site of the original Rothiemurchus hut. Take the path by the bell past a seat and picnic table, and bear right off the track after the table to follow a sign to Lairig Ghru.

The path, which is often damp underfoot, climbs steadily to ● with more wonderful views en route. Turn right on to the Lairig Ghru and retrace your steps to the Cairngorm Club Footbridge. Photographers will appreciate the beauty of Lochan Deò, passed just before you turn right ● to return to Whitewell. ●

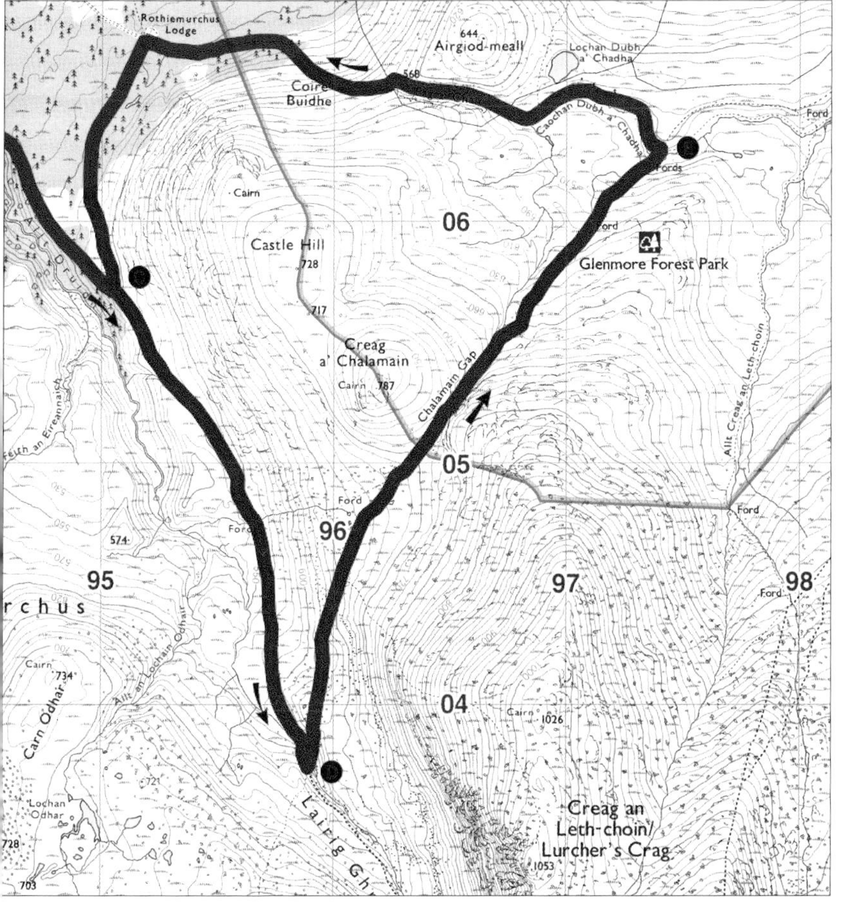

Lochnagar and Loch Muick

Start	Spittal of Glen Muick
Distance	14 miles (22.5km)
Approximate time	7 hours
Parking	At Spittal of Glen Muick car park, at the end of the public road through Glen Muick from Ballater
Refreshments	None
Ordnance Survey maps	Landranger 44 (Ballater & Glen Clova), Explorer 388 (Lochnagar, Glen Muick & Glen Clova)

This long walk (including a climb of about 2000ft/610m) may be shortened by returning along the north west shore of Loch Muick from Glas-allt-Shiel. Lochnagar is a monarch of mountains even though its summit (3786ft/1155m) is modest compared to some neighbours. This is forgotten at the summit, overlooking the grandest of all corries and a landscape that comprises almost half of Scotland. The Lochnagar massif covers 63 sq miles (163 sq km) with 11 tops over 3000ft (914m). The precipitous drops on its eastern side have claimed many lives so it is very important to have a favourable weather forecast and good outdoor clothing, plus a map and compass.

■ Walk from the car park past the information point and turn right following the waymark on to the Lochnagar path. This crosses the river and there is an enticing glimpse of vertical rock faces framed by folds in the hills. When the path comes to the driveway for Allt-na-giubhsaich **A** take the signposted path between the trees (left) and the stable block of the lodge (right), initially following electricity lines to cross a bridge and enter woodland. Allt-na-giubhsaich was used by Queen Victoria as a 'cottage' where she and Prince Albert would come to escape the formalities of life at Balmoral, attended by just a handful of servants.

There is an attractive short length of path which winds through trees before it reaches a Land Rover track which takes the route out of woodland and on to the open hill. A mile or so of straightforward walking follows as the track climbs steadily up to the watershed, passing above the ravine named Clais Rathadan. The top of the col is at 2224ft (678m) and the track turns north to descend Glen Gelder. However, the Lochnagar route is to the left here **B**, marked by a cairn, on a path which heads westwards. About 80 minutes of walking will bring you to this point.

The well repaired path climbs towards the gap between the conical Meikle Pap on the right and the more irregular Cuidhe Crom on the left. A rectangular block set on top of a boulder to the left of the path may catch your eye. This is a memorial to Bill Stuart who died on Lochnagar on 16 August 1953. It is sited by a spring named the Fox Cairn Well, and you will need to make the most of its waters if the day is warm as this is the last spring passed on the way up.

Take care not to climb right to the top of the col but look for a zigzag path to the left ● which climbs more steeply up a rocky staircase appropriately known as The Ladder. *Care is needed here as the surface has become eroded.* If you continue up the other path to the col you will be rewarded by a fine view of the Lochnagar corrie but will either have to return to The Ladder or undertake an unpleasant climb over boulders to rejoin the correct path higher up.

Once on top of the summit plateau take the path which leads to the peaks a safe distance from the edge of the corrie – this is well marked by cairns.

The Red Spout is a point where the rocky edge ends and a funnel of red earth seems to lead directly down to the loch about 600ft (183m) below. Certainly on this initial stretch of the plateau it is important to stay away from the edge, if only to make certain of where the return path leaves. There is a short stretch where the path climbs through a narrow, rocky defile. The homeward path leaves south eastwards immediately after this ● and you can see it below following the course of the Glas Allt, a small burn at first but a more substantial stream later when it plunges down to Loch Muick.

The path becomes broader after ● and soon reaches Cac Carn Mor where there is a large cairn. However, this is not the summit even though the cliffs here give breathtaking views of the corrie. The true summit is about 1/4 mile (400m) farther on to

The falls on the Glas Allt

the north west, a rocky tor capped by a trig point and a mountain indicator dating from 1924. This is Cac Carn Beag, which confusingly (and politely) translates as 'the cairn of the little heap of manure'. The mountain indicator (which is ceramic) shows points from Ben Nevis and Ben Lomond, to the Caithness and Pentland Hills. On a really clear day you can see The Cheviot whose ridge forms the border with England. However, the chief impression is of wilderness where there are few features recognisable as being the works of man.

Lochnagar has inspired many writers including Lord Byron. References abound in his work and his *Lachin y Gair* ends:

'England! Thy beauties are tame and domestic
To one who has roved o'er the mountains afar!
Oh, for the crags that are wild and majestic!
The steep frowning glories of dark Loch na Garr.'

Once you have enjoyed the view from here, return to ● and instead of turning left go straight ahead on the twisting path down towards the Glas Allt ('the green burn'). The dark cliffs above Loch Muick can be seen ahead

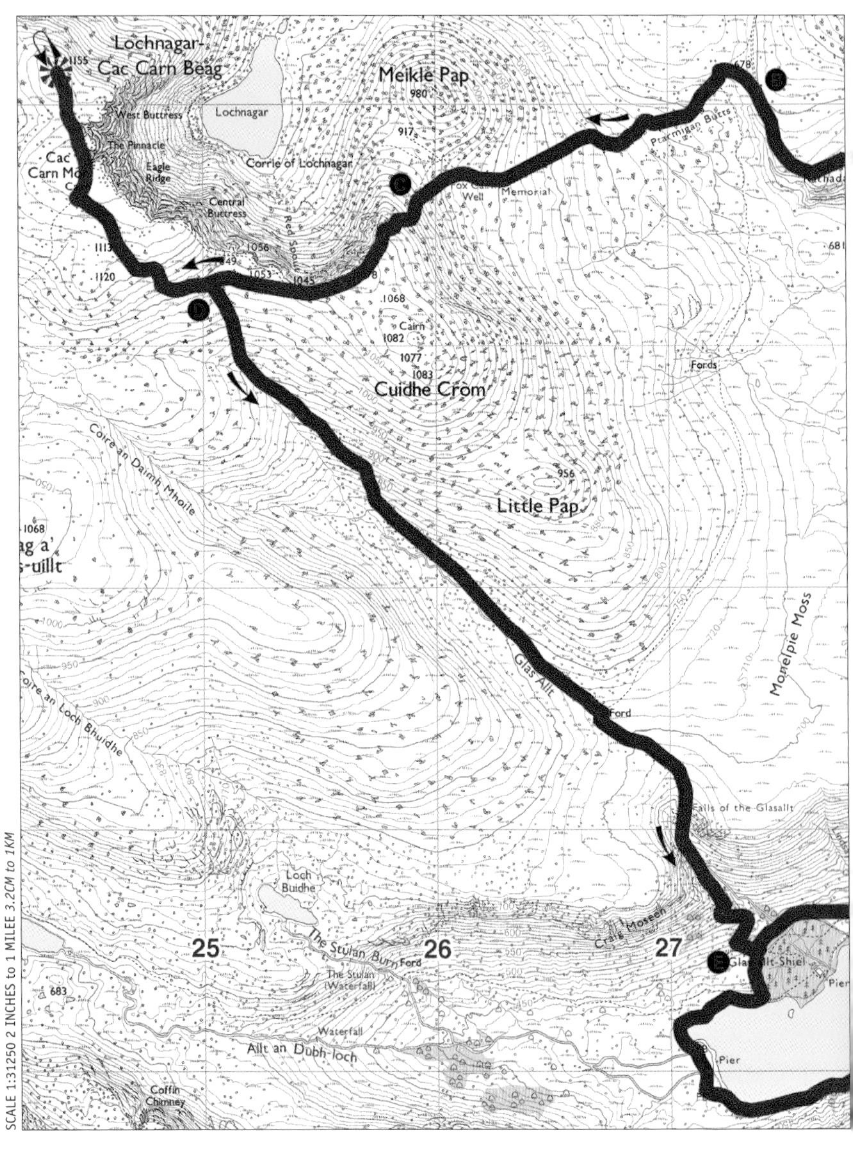

but there is no sight of the loch itself. The path crosses to the south west bank of the burn over a wooden footbridge and a delightful part of the descent follows with the stream close to the left. Soon there are small cataracts – forerunners of the Glas Allt Falls – and Loch Muick comes into view. The main waterfall has a drop of about 70ft (21m) and is well seen from the narrow path.

When the path reaches the woods which surround Glas-allt-Shiel go through the old stone wall and turn right ● through the woods. However, if you are tired at this point it would be better to cross the Glas Allt by the wooden bridge just below ● and then follow the path to the drive on the north west shore of the loch. Follow the drive and turn right by a

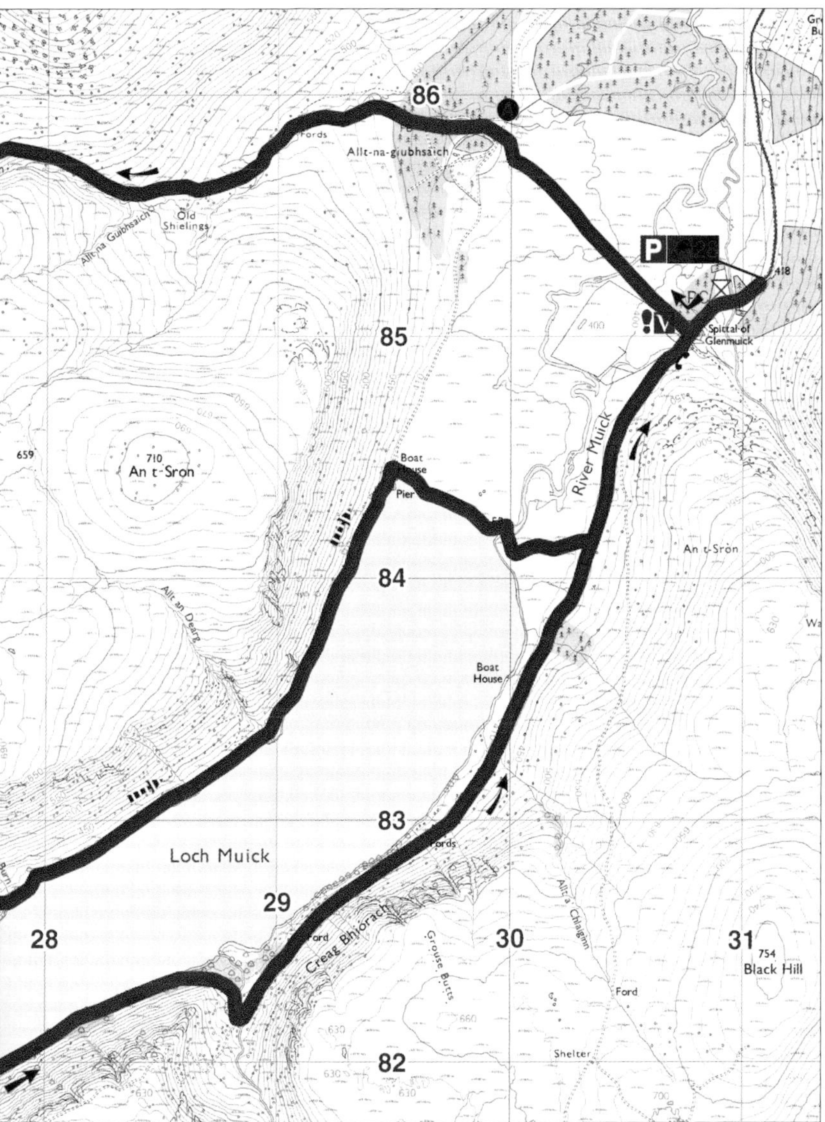

boathouse at the lower end of the loch on to a good path which leads to the popular lochside path from the information centre.

The longer route entails going round the top end of Loch Muick to reach the path seen earlier following the shoreline. At the corner of the wood descend over logs laid on boggy ground to reach the lochside path and turn right. There is a sandy beach by the footbridge over the Allt an Dubh-loch just before you reach this path. A $3^1/_2$-mile (5.5km) walk back to the Spittal of Glenmuick from this point is constantly delightful, the scenery encompassing views across the loch with Creag a' Ghlas-uillt occasionally seen above the steep slopes facing the loch. After crossing the Black Burn the views back are stunning in the evening light and make a grand finale to a memorable day on the hills. ●

Further Information

The Law and Tradition as they affect Walking in Scotland

Walkers following the routes given in this book should not run into problems, but it is as well to know something about the law as it affects access, and also something of the traditions which can be quite different in Scotland from elsewhere in Britain. Most of this is common sense, observing the country code and having consideration for other people and their activities which, after all, may be their livelihood.

It is often said that there is no law of trespass in Scotland. In fact there is, but the trespass itself is not usually a criminal offence. You can be asked to leave any property, and technically 'reasonable force' may be used to obtain your compliance – though the term is not defined! You can be charged with causing damage due to the trespass, but this would be hard to establish if you were just walking on open, wild, hilly country where, whatever the law, in practice there has been a long tradition of free access for recreational walking – something both the Scottish Landowners' Federation and the Mountaineering Council of Scotland do not want to see changed.

There are certain restrictions. Walkers should obey the country code and seasonal restrictions arising from lambing or stalking. Where there is any likelihood of such restrictions this is mentioned in the text and visitors are asked to comply. When camping, use a campsite. Camp fires should not be lit; they are a danger to moorland and forest, and really not necessary as lightweight and efficient stoves are now available.

Many of the walks in this book are on rights of way. The watchdog on rights of way in Scotland is the Scottish Rights of Way Society (SRWS), who maintain details on all established cases and will, if need be, contest attempted closures. They produce a booklet on the Scottish legal position *(Rights of Way, A Guide to the Law in Scotland, 1991)*, and their green signposts are a familiar sight by many footpaths and tracks, indicating the lines of historic routes.

In Scotland rights of way are not marked on Ordnance Survey maps as is the case south of the border. It was not felt necessary to show these as such on the maps – a further reflection of the freedom to roam that is enjoyed in Scotland. So a path on a map is no indication of a right of way, and many paths and tracks of great use to walkers were built by estates as stalking paths or for private access. While you may traverse such paths, taking due care to avoid damage to property and the natural environment, you should obey restricted access notices and leave if asked to do so.

The only established rights of way are those where a court case has resulted in a legal judgment, but there are thousands of other 'claimed' rights of way. Local planning authorities have

Waterfalls in the Linn of Quoich

a duty to protect rights of way – no easy task with limited resources. Many attempts at closing claimed rights of way have been successfully contested in the courts by the Scottish Rights of Way Society and local authorities.

A dog on a lead or under control may also be taken on a right of way. There is little chance of meeting a free-range solitary bull on any of the walks. Any herds seen are not likely to be dairy cattle, but all cows can be inquisitive and may approach walkers, especially if they have a dog. Dogs running among stock may be shot on the spot; this is not draconian legislation but a desperate attempt to stop sheep and lambs being harmed, driven to panic or lost, sometimes with fatal results. Any practical points or restrictions applicable will be made in the text. If there is no comment it can be assumed that the route carries no real restrictions.

Scotland in fact likes to keep everything as natural as possible, so, for instance, waymarking is kept to a minimum (the Scottish Rights of Way Society signposts and Forest Walk markers are in unobtrusive colours). In Scotland people are asked to 'walk softly in the wilderness, to take nothing except photographs, and leave nothing except footprints' – which is better than any law.

Scotland's Hills and Mountains: a Concordat on Access

This remarkable agreement was published early in 1996 and is likely to have considerable influence on walkers' rights in Scotland in the future. The signatories include organisations which have formerly been at odds - the Scottish Landowners' Federation and the Ramblers' Association, for example. However they joined with others to make the Access Forum (a full list of signatories is detailed below). The RSPB (who hold much of the high ground of the Cairngorm plateau) and the National Trust for Scotland (the new owners of the Mar Lodge Estate) did not sign the Concordat initially but it is hoped that they will support its principles.

The signatories of the Concordat are:

Association of Deer Management Groups
Convention of Scottish Local Authorities
Mountaineering Council of Scotland
National Farmers' Union of Scotland
Ramblers' Association Scotland
Scottish Countryside Activities Council
Scottish Landowners' Federation
Scottish Natural Heritage
Scottish Sports Association
Scottish Sports Council

They agreed that the basis of access to the hills for the purposes of informal recreation should be:

- Freedom of access exercised with responsibility and subject to reasonable constraints for management and conservation purposes.
- Acceptance by visitors of the needs of land management, and understanding of how this sustains the livelihood, culture and community interests of those who live and work in the hills.
- Acceptance by land managers of the public's expectation of having access to the hills.
- Acknowledgment of a common interest in the natural beauty and special qualities of Scotland's hills, and the need to work together for their protection and enhancement.

The Forum point out that the success of the Concordat will depend on all who manage or visit the hills acting on these four principles. In addition, the parties to the Concordat will promote good practice in the form of:

- Courtesy and consideration at a personal level.
- A welcome to visitors.

- Making advice readily available on the ground or in advance.
- Better information about the uplands and hill land uses through environmental education.
- Respect by visitors for the welfare needs of livestock and wildlife.
- Adherence to relevant codes and standards of good practice by visitors and land managers alike.
- Any local restrictions on access should be essential for the needs of management, should be fully explained, and be for the minimum period and area required.

Queries should be addressed to: Access Forum Secretariat, c/o Recreation and Access Branch, Scottish Natural Heritage, 2 Anderson Place, Edinburgh EH6 5NP.

Visitors and the Mountain Environment – a note from the RSPB

The high Cairngorms are outstandingly important for the extent and variety of their habitats and associated flora and fauna. It is now widely accepted that some of the high level routes described in this guide cross areas where the soils and vegetation are especially fragile. Here, even relatively modest use of the ground by people can lead to damage. The severe climate and thin infertile soils mean that recovery of damaged areas will be very slow and uncertain. The large number of people who visit Cairn Gorm and the wider mountain area, encouraged by the easy access provided by the ski road, car park and chairlift, has resulted in extensive loss of soils and vegetation.

In part as a response to these pressures a wide range of landowners and special interest groups have formed the Cairn Gorm Tourism Management Programme.

A number of management principles have been defined. The key one, in the context of this guide book, is that numbers of visitors reaching the summit of Cairn Gorm should not increase beyond current levels and that on the plateau between Cairn Gorm and Ben Macdui, and in the northern corries, numbers should be reduced. The aim is to prevent further damage to habitats and to allow for sustained recovery.

Targets for the level of reductions and mechanisms to achieve them have yet to be agreed. However, the Tourism Management Programme Group intends that visitor management initiatives will be implemented over the coming years. In the mean time, when walking the high level routes suggested in this guide, please endeavour to heed the Cairngorm Code.

Cairngorm Code

Avoid disturbing wildlife:

- go quietly so you do not disturb birds and animals
- do not pick any flowers or plants
- try to keep to well marked paths
- if your dog is with you keep it close to you

Leave the mountain undamaged:

- do not go higher than you need to
- keep to the middle of paths and do not take short cuts
- do not move rocks

Improve the appearance of the Cairngorms:

- take your litter home
- reduce erosion by keeping to paths
- walk in single file so people have room to pass

Look after your own safety:

- remember that storms can blow up very suddenly at any time of year
- wear suitable clothes and footwear
- have map and compass with you at all times.

Safety on the Hills

The Highland hills and lower but remote areas call for care and respect. The idyllic landscape of the tourist

The Chalamain Gap in winter

brochures can change rapidly into a world of gales, rain and mist, potentially lethal for those ill-equipped or lacking navigational skills. The Scottish hills in winter can be arctic in severity, and even in summer, snow can lash the summits.

At the very least carry adequate wind- and waterproof outer garments, food and drink to spare, a basic first-aid kit, whistle, map and compass – and know how to use them. Wear boots. Plan within your capabilities. If going alone ensure you leave details of your proposed route. Heed local advice, listen to weather forecasts, and do not hesitate to modify plans if conditions deteriorate.

Some of the walks in this book venture into remote country and others climb high summits, and these expeditions should only be undertaken in good summer conditions. In winter they could well need the skills and experience of mountaineering rather than walking. In midwinter the hours of daylight are of course much curtailed, but given crisp, clear late-winter days many of the shorter expeditions would be perfectly feasible, if the guidelines given are adhered to.

Mountain Rescue

In case of emergency the standard procedure is to dial 999 and ask for the police who will assess and deal with the situation.

First, however, render first aid as required and make sure the casualty is made warm and comfortable. The distress signal (six flashes/whistle-blasts, repeated at minute intervals) may bring help from other walkers in the area. Write down essential details: exact location (six-figure reference), time of accident, numbers involved, details of injuries, steps already taken; then despatch a messenger to phone the police.

If leaving the casualty alone, mark the site with an eye-catching object. Be patient; waiting for help can seem interminable.

Useful Organisations

Association for the Protection of Rural Scotland

Gladstone's Land, 3rd floor,
483 Lawnmarket,
Edinburgh EH1 2NT.
Tel. 0131 225 7012

Forestry Commission Scotland
Silvan House,
231 Corstorphine Road,
Edinburgh EH12 7AT.
Tel. 0131 334 0303

Historic Scotland
Longmore House, Salisbury Place,
Edinburgh EH9 1SH.
Tel. 0131 668 8600

Long Distance Walkers' Association
Bank House, High Street, Wrotham,
Sevenoaks, Kent TN15 7AE.
Tel. 01732 883705

Mountaineering Council of Scotland
The Old Granary, West Mill Street,
Perth PH1 5QP.
Tel. 01738 638227
www.mountaineering-scotland.org.uk

Glossary of Gaelic Names

Most of the place names in this region are Gaelic in origin, and this list gives some of the more common elements, which will allow readers to understand otherwise meaningless words and appreciate the relationship between place names and landscape features. Place names often have variant spellings, and the more common of these are given here.

aber	mouth of loch, river
abhainn	river
allt	stream
auch, ach	field
bal, bail, baile	town, homestead
bàn	white, fair, pale
bealach	hill pass
beg, beag	small
ben, beinn	hill
bhuidhe	yellow
blar	plain
brae, braigh	upper slope, steepening
breac	speckled
cairn	pile of stones, often marking a summit
cam	crooked
càrn	cairn, cairn-shaped hill
caol, kyle	strait
ceann, ken, kin	head
cil, kil	church, cell
clach	stone
clachan	small village
cnoc	hill, knoll, knock
coille, killie	wood
corrie, coire, choire	mountain hollow
craig, creag	cliff, crag
crannog, crannag	man-made island
dàl, dail	field, flat
damh	stag
dearg	red
druim, drum	long ridge
dubh, dhu	black, dark
dùn	hill fort
eas	waterfall
eilean	island
eilidh	hind
eòin, eun	bird
fionn	white
fraoch	heather
gabhar, ghabhar, gobhar	goat
garbh	rough
geal	white
ghlas, glas	grey
gleann, glen	narrow, valley
gorm	blue, green
inbhir, inver	confluence
inch, inis, innis	island, meadow by river
lag, laggan	hollow
làrach	old site
làirig	pass
leac	slab
liath	grey
loch	lake
lochan	small loch
màm	pass, rise
maol	bald-shaped top
monadh	upland, moor
mór, mor(e)	big
odhar, odhair	dun-coloured
rhu, rubha	point
ruadh	red, brown
sgòr, sgòrr, sgùrr	pointed
sron	nose
stob	pointed
strath	valley (broader than glen)
tarsuinn	traverse, across
tom	hillock (rounded)
tòrr	hillock (more rugged)
tulloch, tulach	knoll
uisge	water, river

National Trust for Scotland
Wemyss House, 28 Charlotte Square,
Edinburgh EH2 4ET.
Tel. 0131 243 9300

Ordnance Survey
Romsey Road, Maybush,
Southampton SO16 4GU.
Tel. 08456 05 05 05 (Lo-call)

Ramblers' Association (Scotland)
Kingfisher House, Auld Mart Business Park, Milnathort, Kinross KY13 9DA.
Tel. 01577 861222

Royal Society for the Protection of Birds Scotland HQ
Dunedin House, 25 Ravelston Terrace,
Edinburgh EH4 3TP.
Tel. 0131 311 6500
www.rspb.org.uk

Scottish Landowners' Federation
Stuart House, Eskmill Business Park,
Musselburgh, EH21 7PB.
Tel. 0131 653 5400

Scottish Natural Heritage
12 Hope Terrace, Edinburgh EH9 2AS.
Tel. 0131 447 4784

Scottish Rights of Way & Access Society
24 Annandale Street,
Edinburgh EH7 4AN.
Tel. 0131 558 1222
www.scotways.com

Scottish Wildlife Trust
Cramond House, Cramond Glebe Road,
Edinburgh EH4 6NS.
Tel. 0131 312 7765
www.swt.org.uk

Scottish Youth Hostels Association
7 Glebe Crescent, Stirling FK8 2JA.
Tel. 0870 155 3255
www.syha.org.uk

Tourist information:
Scottish Tourist Board
23 Ravelston Terrace, Edinburgh EH4 3EU.
Tel. 0131 332 2433
www.holiday.scotland.net

Highlands of Scotland Tourist Board
Peffery House,
Strathpeffer IV14 9HA.
Tel. 01997 421160

Tourist Information Centres
Local tourist information numbers:
Aviemore: 01479 810363
Ballater: 013397 55306
Braemar: 013397 41600
Crathie: 013397 42414
Grantown-on-Spey: 01479 872773
Kingussie: 01540 661297
Tomintoul: 01807 580285

Ordnance Survey Maps of the Cairngorms

The walks described in this guide are covered by Ordnance Survey 1:50,000 scale (1¼ inches to 1 mile or 2cm to 1km) Landranger map sheets 35, 36, 37, 43, 44, 52.

These all-purpose maps are packed with information to help you explore the area. Viewpoints, picnic sites, places of interest and caravan and camping sites are shown, as well as public rights of way information such as footpaths and bridleways.

To examine this area in more detail, especially if you are planning walks, the Ordnance Survey Explorer maps at 1:25 000 scale (2½ inches to 1 mile or 4cm to 1km) are ideal:

387 Glen Shee & Braemar
388 Lochnagar, Glen Muick & Glen Clova
402 Badenoch & Upper Strathspey
403 Cairngorm & Aviemore
404 Braemar, Tomintoul, Glen Avon
405 Aboyne, Alford & Strathdon
419 Grantown-on-Spey & Hills of Cromdale

To get to the Cairngorms use the Ordnance Survey OS Travel Map-Route Great Britain at 1:625 000 scale (4cm to 25km or 1 inch to 10 miles) or Ordnance Survey OS Travel Map-Road 1 (Northern Scotland, Orkney and Shetland) at 1:250 000 scale (1cm to 2.5km or 1 inch to 4 miles).

Ordnance Survey maps and guides are available from most booksellers, stationers and newsagents.

www.totalwalking.co.uk

www.totalwalking.co.uk
is the official website of the Jarrold Pathfinder and Short Walks guides. This interactive website features a wealth of information for walkers – from the latest news on route diversions and advice from professional walkers to product news, free sample walks and promotional offers.

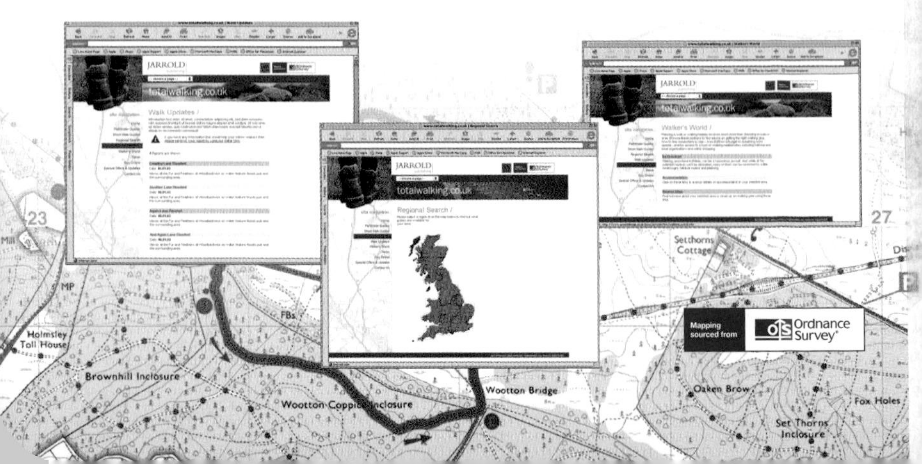